Trade Secrets of a Seer

Trade Secrets of a Seer ~ How Jesus Taught Me to Speak Life Back Into My Life Even When…

Keeping Your Head Above Water in Hard Times by

Denise Rand Dahlheimer

Trade Secrets of a Seer

## Copyright (c) 2022 – Denise Rand Dahlheimer

All right reserved. No portion of this book may be reproduced, stored in a retrieval system, or transmitted in any form or by any means, electronic, mechanical, photocopying, recording, or otherwise, without express written permission of this publisher. Published by Denise Rand Dahlheimer's Meet Me in the Mountains, LLC and is a registered trademark, pending. It is illegal to copy this book, post it on any website, or distribute it by any other means without the permission of the author.

Denise Rand Dahlheimer asserts the moral right to be identified as the author of this work.

Scripture quotations are taken from the Holy Bible; KJV, NKJV, and NIV versions are trademarks registered to the United States Patent and Trademark Office by Biblical, Inc. The characters and events portrayed in this book are fictitious and any similarity to real persons, living or deceased, is coincidental. If you know me, you know.

Author: Denise Rand Dahlheimer

Address: Silver Creek Township, Maple Lake, MN 55358

ArtOnTheOutskirts@yahoo.com

# Trade Secrets of a Seer

# Trade Secrets of a Seer

## Table of Contents

Prologue ...................................................................................... v
Dedication ................................................................................. vii
Acknowledgment ..................................................................... viii
About the Author ....................................................................... xi
Secret Number 1 – Find Jesus! .................................................... 1

    Pray the Salvation Prayer .......................................................9

Secret Number 2 – Pray in Jesus' Name ..................................... 12
Secret Number 3 – Meet the Holy Spirit ................................... 16

    Pray for Guidance ................................................................. 17

Secret Number 4 – It is in How You Ask .................................. 29
Secret Number 5 – Faith over Fear ........................................... 36

    The Resurrection Prayer ....................................................... 46

    Ask for God's Anointing ....................................................... 47

Secret Number 6 - Loopholes & Opinions ................................ 48
Secret Number 7 - The Spiritual Realm .................................... 54
Secret Number 8 – Choose Whom You Serve ........................... 72
Secret Number 9 - Forgiveness Heals ....................................... 80
Secret Number 10 – Don't Get Left Behind .............................. 99

    The Sinner's Prayer ............................................................ 100

Author Bio .............................................................................. 109
About the Cover ..................................................................... 113
Credits & Concordance .......................................................... 115

**About the Cover**

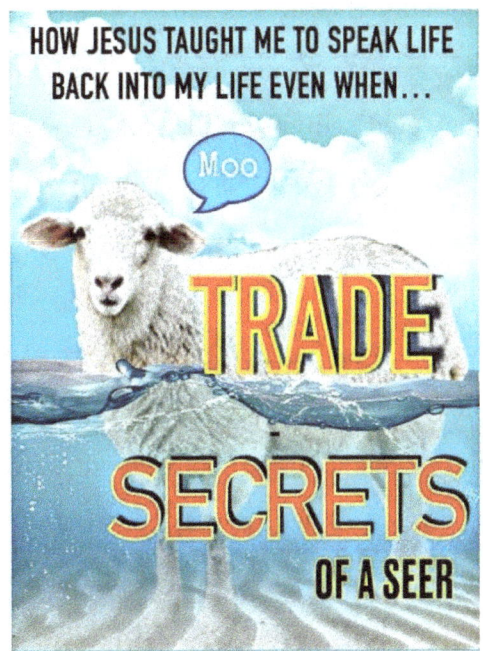

The United States Patent and Trademark Office refers to a trade secret as a type of intellectual property that provides a competitive edge.

Secrets in the Heavenly realm are a contradiction to this. God says in the Bible, "that when you seek me with your whole heart, you will find me," and it is no secret. The way is laid out open and free to all who want it. As a seer, just as described by the Evangelist Bob Jones, "You can discern what's going in with people through their incense. You can do it with your taste: "Taste and see that the Lord is good" per Psalms 34:8. You can do it through your feelings, sight, and things you hear… People think you're loony because of your revelation and dreams and how God communicates with you. But when churches reject you, they're bidding goodbye to their own mercy.

As a seer, you are there for mercy. You are there to help bring healing to the people and show them what God is doing. It is time for the seer to come forth. The church needs you. It is time for the seer to mature and be used."

As a seer, my reality is that God's divine principles are not limited. And as His child, I look at my circumstances with my feet planted firmly on the rock, Jesus, while choosing the attitude of gratitude that keeps my head above the water of troubles.

Worldly success defines "more" as being better. Be it an ultra-car wash or a supersized dinner, to upgrade an automobile, a bigger home, better clothes, etc., we have been set up to focus on what we do not have. That all lack must be filled. When we pray for what we do not have, natural law dictates that we will surely receive more lack, as that is where our attention lies. This is referred to as the Baader-Meinhof phenomenon, more commonly known as "the red car syndrome," where once we notice a red car, all we then see are red cars, like an ear-worm. Reality is not altered; there aren't more red cars, but our attention says there are. If we focus on what we do not have, our focus will be consumed by what we do not have. In this state, all joy and happiness evaporate.

An attitude of gratitude for what God has blessed us with changes this outcome. As we pray with a thankful heart and thanking Jesus for the troubles we encounter, it may sound as crazy as a sheep bleating "moo," but it is the most innovative way to end them.

Live the verse in 1 Thessalonians 5:18, "In everything give thanks: for this is the will of God in Christ Jesus concerning you."

I may not walk on water as Jesus did, but I can stay afloat while waiting for His return. ~Denise

## Prologue

"Get up. Take your mat. And go home." Jesus said to the paralyzed man. I get it. I can choose despair, or I can choose hope. I can choose illness, or I can choose to heal. I can choose how I want my life to play out.

The Book of Mark Chapter 2 tells the story of the paralyzed man whose friends went to great lengths to take him to Jesus. When Jesus saw the effort they put forth, He said, "Son, your sins are forgiven." This outraged the local authorities, who were already in a coup d'etat to negate His authority. Jesus not only dismissed these teachers' charges, but He did one better than just forgiving the man; He healed him as well. Why? Because illness in any form is not of God. It is a perversion of everything about God. And interesting side note... the man was healed because of the faith of his friends.

The devil wishes for us to be crippled from an abundant life and is clever enough to get us to think it is all legit. From crippling ideas or situations to not making a move, to fighting the urge to make the call, to not do the thing, to stick with what we know out of comfort or fear, to not gift, to not relinquish, to not give in, to not back down, to not give a second chance, to refuse to see "it" from "their" point of view, to hang on to ideals, or to have hidden our love of Jesus rather than risk being heckled.

I learned the secrets of winning over losing. I learned to build my nest in crashing waves. I realized anyone could survive, so I went for thriving! I realized God keeps His promise that when I am weak, He is strong. With Him backing me, I chose life in abundance. I stopped looking at what was wrong, and He opened my eyes to what is right. As one of God's children, I kept a distance from self-pity as it sabotages my hopes. I learned I had to make the first move, a step of faith.

The Bible says in Jeremiah 29:13, "And you will seek Me and find Me when you search for Me with all your heart." And as I did with Jesus guiding Me up and over the mountains, I discovered the real secrets of success. And I will see you on the other side! So let me tell you what I have found out! And thank you for being here. Blessings!

## Dedication

I dedicate Trade Secrets of Seer to my mother, Gloria Jeane, whose training to be who and what I am has allowed me to know that I can hop up on God's lap anytime and ask Him to "fix it please." Her acceptance of my God-given gifts, much like her own, caused my life to exceed my wildest dreams. And to my dad, Gordy, who taught me that it takes balance to move forward. Our time as a family was cut short, but I remember us every day. I know your lives, like mine, are in God's hands per Job 14:5, "Since his days are determined, The number of his months is with You; You have appointed his limits so that he cannot pass."

Through you, I learned to not accept the limits of "good enough" and to instead choose the freedom in "it is good," which caused an atmosphere I can thrive in. This is my gift to you.

And I dedicate this to my Lord Jesus, for whom I am literally eternally grateful in so many ways. I love you. Thank you for the life you have given me.

## Acknowledgment

I wish to acknowledge my husband, who, when in the early stages of our dating, I once asked you for a favor, not even a split second passed before you said, "Yes, in a heartbeat." No questions were asked. No deals were made. You just went all in. I realized right then and there that you are a man who understands how to love without reserve. And 32 years in, you have never let me down once. You also went all in and became "dad" and "pops" to my teen children and are a true bridge builder. Thank you, my love, for being the "best is yet to come." Because our lives have always been punctuated by music, the song <u>Smile, by Uncle Kracker</u> sums it up best when he sings…

"You make me smile like the sun. Fall out of bed, sing like a bird.
Dizzy in my head, spin like a record.
Crazy on a Sunday night you make me dance like a fool.
Forget how to breathe Shine like gold, buzz like a bee.
Just the thought of you can drive me wild Oh, you make me smile…"

You truly are cooler than the flip side of my pillow. My heart flutters every time I look at you. Thank you for being you. I love you.

I would also like to acknowledge my son. As I look back on the photos we accumulated in our story, I see lots of good times, lots of fun, lots of eye contact, lots of talking. In my heart, I see what my choices did to you, and I will grieve them for the rest of my life. When I finally gathered God unto me enough to make the changes we needed to live, I prayed it was not too late. I trust Jesus to continually care for you and I know that where there is Jesus, there is healing. And with Him, it is a given that we all heal.

And just like your dad, there is a song that plays in my heart for you. When you were in the Iraqi war, you once called me at work from the Gulf, and we had such a good talk. And you told me that you listened to a song that Ozzy Osbourne sang, and I did not understand all that you were telling me in it as I only heard "Mama, I am coming home." It was all I wanted to hear. But the lyrics say…

"Times have changed and times are strange.

Here I come, but I ain't the same.

Mama, I'm coming home. Times gone by seeming to be

You could have been a better friend to me Mama, I'm coming home…"

I see your face in my heart every time I close my eyes, and I look upon it with love. I am incredibly proud of you, and I thank God you were born into my life. In the next one, I promise it will be easier. You always matter to me. I love you. My heart is always yours.

To my daughter, you know the story of how Wonderful World by Louis Armstrong is in my top five songs of all time, but you never asked why. In the late 1960s, this song was the product to be released by Mr. Armstrong to bring peace to a war-torn world. The lyrics…

"I see trees of green, red roses too. I see them bloom for you and me. And I think to myself, what a wonderful world."

This is all about you. This is why God brought you into my life. You were a gift of the sweetest roses to my war-torn life. You brought and still bring much-needed color and beauty to my black and white world. I thank God for you! You matter. I am so incredibly proud of you as I watch you bloom and grow, and I love you with all my heart. Your very being here blesses me.

To all of you, May the Lord bless you and keep you. May He make His face shine upon you. May He give you peace and hold you close always. In Jesus' Name, Amen. You are proof that good things do come in threes.

## About the Author

Born an artist and a seer, Denise tells the stories of her walk with Jesus and shares her "secrets" to answered prayers.

Trade Secrets of a Seer

## Secret Number 1 – Find Jesus!

I was born an artist and a seer. I recall coloring everything! Blank surfaces still call out to me. Lol! I like long walks on a warm sandy beach, traveling, and holding hands with my husband—we both like big dogs, early mornings, and our kids. I like creating art on and beyond the canvas, and the Holy Spirit tasked me to blog the stories of my paintings and our adventures with Jesus. I grew up seeing the supernatural, and I love to tell the stories of how Jesus interacts in my life.

Ecclesiastes states, "To everything, there is a season, and a time to every purpose under heaven: A time to be born…" Yes, I was born to see with spiritual eyes and perceive the supernatural world. I knew I was blessed to have an ambidextrous type of brain, and this was nurtured and mentored with a Christian upbringing from my earliest memory. When telling my parents of the old guy spirit walking in slippers down the stairs, it was often met with, "okay, but did you clean your room yet?"

This attitude of disregard allowed me to disregard the dark side stuff as I focused my attention on the good things of Jesus. It gave me a solid foundation of just how big God is. As with all people, hurts happened and left their mark. Though these marks may have stalled me, they did not end me. But in hindsight, I see where I took Jesus for granted.

As an artistic child, my world was a regular routine of family, school, play, and church to which we showed up every week, sang the songs, prayed the prayers, calling it good for another week. As the artist within grew into my teen years, where the rebellious nature reigns as queen, I spent most of my school time in the art room. My parents were often gone out saving the world, and I was left behind at home. I retaliated with smoking, drinking, and partying. One evening, bored, I recall watching the local Evangelical Pastor on television. The hymn, I Believe in Miracles by Carlton Buck, played as the show was opening. And then they offered a poster of a butterfly in metamorphosis in return for a donation, both of which caught my attention, and I sent for it. The poster soon arrived, and it spoke to my soul. It was my first experience of "experiencing" a picture. It was incredibly prophetic.

And then dun-dun-dunnnn... I met a guy, "My soul mate," and I loved him with all my immature 17 years, and he loved me back. But something was off. But, the same something said we were "destined" to be. Was it God?

Maybe. Was it of evil? No. But evil will soon play its hand. When I first painted his portrait in the high school art room, a light flickered in the back of my thoughts about this relationship. The painting depicted a frontal view overlaid by an obscured profile. I became aware, too late, that this was an honest-to-God kind of prophetic works depiction of a split persona. Yeah but... I was pregnant. I finished high school, and we moved in together, which started a cycle of beatings and apologies, and I "knew" I couldn't go home; the parents had rented out my room. And because I came from a "good" family, the forced wedding happened. Even though I wore black to it, I wanted this baby, I cared my best for the fetus within me, and I loved this boy I married.

But something else was off—unseen things. And even my paintings began to bear a black aura. There were so many fights, real and surreal. I saw literal demons prowling my small yard and peering in my windows. I watched as the beautiful brown eyes of the boy I had loved transformed into those of a wolf. Our toddler cried all the time, and our new baby rarely slept. No, there was no peace in this home. So many times, I cried out to Jesus for His forgiveness for being so stupid. I begged for His mercy and asked Him to protect my children. I asked Him to be strong in me as I was now helpless as I kneeled on the worn carpet and cried. I cried out of physical pain. I cried for my lost life. I cried because I was turning 20 years old, ready to die. I cried for my babies because I could not. I was their only barrier.

And then there was a "feeling" in the room. I looked up through stinging tears, and there Jesus stood. Glowing. White. Golden hands lifted, reaching out to me as one tear fell down His cheek. In my living room! One tear and I was utterly…what…what was this I was feeling? It feels like devastation. It feels like brokenness. It feels like what…hope? I finally felt unconditional love.

Yes, God had seen when I made my immature teen choice in a mate. He agreed to this change in the plan that had been set forth for me. He saw me as the man/child who bore the thievery of his own childhood upon me in the form of spousal abuse as I bore him two beautiful babies. I understood, and I tried. God had warned me it would be hard but that He would help me every step of the way. He made away. He protected my life as together we protected theirs. I understood.

The song <u>Jesus Loves Me by Anna Warner</u> has always been my anthem song, and I often sang it to ward off the drive-by spiritual attacks that came at me, trying to destroy my peace with a push to insinuate their darkness into my paintings through loopholes in my speech. I had ignorantly opened myself to the dark side through "dabbling" and "curiosity," evil willingly synced itself to the teenage rebel artist rising up within me.

Adding supernatural talents brought hell that much closer and all over my life. Unfortunately, my paintings reflected all of this. Hell is mesmerizingly ugly. I saw the supernatural spiritual warfare going on around me and for me. I saw angels clashing with demons. And it is loud and it is scary. By the way and a word of warning, those who Jesus does not know are not covered in His protection and are fair game for evil. Just sayin'.

As I recall this mountain in my life, what I remember most is the fear I had. I prayed for deliverance from my woes and trusted God to hear me. Evil is real. Spiritual warfare is real. And so is Jesus, and He loves me. The Bible tells me so as a written promise. He showed me in my living room the honesty in the "I love you so much I would die for you" kind of love because He did. Because in God is all truth. And the truth does set you free. The glimmer of gratitude was taking its rightful place back in my heart.

I dreamed that night, a supernatural dream, of my little family's life in 15 years. I was sitting behind the defendant's table in a courtroom. My now 18-year-old son was being told to approach the judge's bench. A verdict was in. He was found guilty on all charges. They convicted him of life in prison without the possibility of parole for the murder of his biological father. The wife-beater. The abuser. I screamed. I wailed in remorse. He turned to face me and said, "keep your tears. You had your chance. You had every chance in the world to leave, to save us, but you were weak. And this is how I am rewarded for protecting you." He had protected me yet again from being beaten and stopped the abuse… forever.

The abuser was dead.

I awoke from this prophetic dream with new clarity. My eyes were wide open, my thinking was clear, and I knew what I needed to do. It was time to go. No more excuses of no money, no more fear of being a single mom, no more fear. I was all in, and I planned our leaving. No one had been murdered, and no one went to jail. I was grateful that I had the chance to change my path. I packed up our life, and this dream became a significant benchmark for the rest of my life. To save all of our lives, I needed to leave.

I chose to start trusting Jesus as much as possible in my current state of frailty, and things began to change. My husband was now rarely home, and the abuse was subsiding. God softened my will to receive my mother's heart for me, and I was reminded that I was indeed still a daddy's girl. But most of all, I was back and ready to be what I was born to be…me. Or so I thought.

There was no flaw in me that God could see. In His eyes, I was worthy of being treated well. There was no looking back as there was nothing to look back on. My paintings were part of that, and I would never again allow the evil one to capture anything on canvas via me. I attended Bible studies with my parents and became a born- again Christian. I learned that my faith was naive as I tied it directly to what I thought was my parent's approval. I knew I had embarrassed them, or was it that I had embarrassed myself? Why did I slap the face of my upbringing? I hadn't. My values were still there, and I was just a young girl who had taken them for granted. When I wandered away from God's face, the evil one was right there, causing me to assume it was a given that God disapproved of me, and as I believed this lie, it instigated the supernatural fight for my soul.

Of course, my parents loved me. If they had been embarrassed by my actions, they moved past it and adored my children. The thought of saying otherwise was a lie planted by evil. To be entirely protected by God, I went holy roller! The supernatural stuff was now only good and all God. We raised my children, and I appreciated being alive. It had been a close call, but God was there, and He was not having any more abuse inflicted upon me, and my life's path turned around upon my baptism in the Holy Spirit, and my soul breathed a sigh of relief.

Jesus waited for me to use my free will to make the conscious decision to shake up my life out of its chaos caused by poor choices and to get honest with God. I knew that not choosing God directly, the option defaulted to evil. But I had one thing to do. First, I made an offering of my life to God. I stood at the top of the hill, and I watched all my art burn.

Every canvas. Every brush. All the paint. It was painful, and I was beside myself with grief. I killed my art. As the last of it smoldered, I wiped my tears, walked into the mobile home, grabbed my babies out of their beds, put them in the loaded-up old car, and we left. And Jesus walked this with us to the rest of our lives.

Like me, there are people worldwide experiencing the love of Jesus as He ministers to them in their dreams, for the Son of God has the power to change a person's heart through dreams, and still, He leaves the choice to us.

Even though "they" have been saying it for eons, we really do live in crazy scary days. And it is all written about in the most terrifying book of all, Revelation, humanity's final battle, the Apocalypse.

Revelation 3:20 states, "Behold, I stand at the door, and knock: if any man hears my voice, and open the door, I will come into him and will sup with him, and he with me." It does not say, "Oh but not you because you did this…" Just get to Jesus. He will help sort it out. It won't matter if the world falls apart or recovers; how are YOU in Jesus? Being "good with God" or relying on "I was baptized as a baby or a teen" or "my gram dedicated me to God" isn't good enough. If you are old enough to make these assumptions, you are old enough to know there is only one way to heaven, and Jesus is our only entry point.

Nobody comes to the Father except through Him. We all have to make a conscious choice for Jesus. Jesus Christ. King of the Jews. Holy Redeemer. Son of God. Yeshua. Hosannah. Emmanuel. And so on. We know the names. We know of Him. We know about Him. But have we learned about living in the power of Him? Yes, He saves our souls for eternal life. He also wants us to live and love knowing that it was good we were born as we each bring our uniqueness to many lives, should we decide to step out of our zones. This book is about my lessons to living in the Power of Jesus, right here, right now.

Jesus Christ is the Son of God. He is the forgiver of our sins, and He died on the cross to redeem us from death. Only through Him can we meet God. And He is still more than that! He died for more than to just forgive us. He died to change us for the better. We need only to cooperate. When we ask Him into our hearts, and into our lives, and make Him Lord of our life, our God will provide – as long as we are in His grace per John 14:23, "Jesus answered and said unto him, If a man loves me, he will keep my words: and my Father will love him, and we will come unto him, and make our abode with him."

The adage 'If I do what I always do, I will get what I always got" applies well here. I learned He could not help with significant improvements in my life or me if I ghost Him with a quick "sorry 'bout that God" and wonder where I last stashed my Bible. I seek His help in everything, and I seek His answers. Where and how do we start this journey? Talk to Him! "Jesus, here I am. Take me and set me free. Help me."

### Pray the Salvation Prayer

"Father, I know that I have broken your laws, and my sins have separated me from you. I am genuinely sorry, and now I want to turn away from my past sinful life toward you. Please forgive me, and help me avoid sinning again. I believe that your son, Jesus Christ, died for my sins, was resurrected from the dead, is alive, and hears my prayer. I invite Jesus to become the Lord of my life, to rule and reign in my heart from this day forward.

Please send your Holy Spirit to help me obey You and to do Your will for the rest of my life.

In Jesus' Name. Amen.

When I was new to following Jesus, I would offer up a prayer like "talk to me, Jesus, then shut my eyes, open the Bible, and point to a verse. Ta-ta-dah!! Yes, sometimes it worked. But the Bible is not a magic eight ball, and this is no time for "Eenie-Meanie-Jelly-Beanie the spirits are about to speak!" I learned I needed to read the Bible and ask the Holy Spirit to help me absorb it. Yes, absorb. I am not saying understanding it, and do not worry; understanding is in the process. However, I did learn in my eight-ball thinking that not only is Psalms in the middle, but it is also in my top five favorite chapters.

Get a Bible and read it every day. Out loud! From Genesis to Revelation and watch your life change. The closer you walk with Jesus, the less of a pinball you will feel like, keep going forward. Keep your balance. Do not let your words trip you. Once you are down, you are monster bait. Sins can be forgiven if asked in time. Stay in the Word! The word is Jesus. Kick the naysayers to the curb, for the ghosts are gone. We are to emulate Ephesians 4:24 "and put on the new self, created to be like God in true righteousness and holiness." We stand up and walk forward, following God's plans for us as laid out in the Bible. He will teach you to speak life back into your life.

And no, Jesus is not religion. Life with Jesus is like preparing for a destination wedding, and we have lots to do before we get there. Keep in mind the part where it is said, "If anyone here knows of any reason why…", that the devil will indeed stand up and have something to say, making it imperative why we need to do keep our eyes on Jesus. How do we do that? We take God at face value. Read the Bible and stand on God's word. Respond with good to evil. Forgive. Love. 1 Corinthians 13 beautifully says, "If I speak in the tongues of men and angels, but have not to love, I am only a resounding gong or a clanging cymbal. If I have the gift of prophecy and can fathom all mysteries and knowledge, and if I have a faith that can move mountains but have not to love, I am nothing."

Being of love is the single most important thing we can do, and it reminds me of when I once overheard a fellow telling another how he and his wife had chosen to raise their son with unyielding strictness to raise him right and following their religion. He complained that all their hard work had alienated this son from their lives. The recipient of this conversation only replied, "in my church, Jesus forgives."

That simple response spoke volumes to me and witnessed my belief that these people crossed my path to send a message from the cross for me. It's all about love. With a dash of grace. And a whole lot of "Nobody gets it right all the time." And did you know that the entire Bible is about our restoration? And Jesus is there for us 100%.

## Secret Number 2 – Pray in Jesus' Name

Signed, sealed, delivered with "In Jesus Name. Amen." These four words are powerful action words rarely used to appreciate their magnitude. Speak the language of love where good dwells, per Ephesians 4:15, "But speaking the truth in love, may grow up into him in all things, which is the head, even Christ:" Give respect to who God is. Make your amens with "In Jesus Name, Amen," knowing that Jesus heard you, for He is always with you. John 14:13, "And whatsoever ye shall ask in my name, that will I do, that the Father may be glorified in the Son." As we come to live with Him and learn how to put His full power into our petitions to God for help, we are no longer limited to spewing random words, adding in His Name as part of a magic spell to produce a self-style desired effect. We will know that the words we speak to God come from a deep and abiding knowledge of who He is within us. A place where words like mercy, gratitude, blessing, serving, etc., are alive and well and manifesting all over our lives. We only need to cooperate in His basic principles.

I learned praying to God will not guarantee what I want, the way I want, or when I want. Then why pray? His answers are better. How? Why? God is Alpha, the beginning, and Omega, the end, and everything in between, He is King of the universe, and it all belongs to Him. He sees it all. Even with the Abrahamic Covenant of the Old Testament where the Lord tells Abraham, "I will make you into a great nation, and I will bless you; I will make your name great, and you will be a blessing. I will bless those who bless you; and whoever curses you I will curse; and all peoples on earth; will be blessed through you." Genesis 12, God knew there would be a need for the New Testament. He knew that we needed the savior, Jesus Christ, and the counselor, The Holy Spirit, to save us from ourselves, counseling us to live in a state of grace.

The "tate of grace begins with as Jesus declared in Mark 12:30, "And thou shalt love the Lord thy God with all thy heart, and with all thy soul, and with all thy mind, and all thy strength: this is the first commandment." And Mark 12:31, "And the second is like, namely this, thou shalt love thy neighbor as thyself. There is none other commandment greater than these." If we do this, then the world is our oyster, for we ride with the King who owns the term "carte blanche."

That being said, it was not hard to see it was not in my best interest to read the horoscope, consult the stars, and universal vibrations on the one hand and then ask for God to get me a better house, fill the cupboards, or grant healings, or even spare my child on the other. The Bible says in Matthew 6:24, "No man can serve two masters: for either he will hate the one, and love the other; or else he will hold to the one, and despise the other. Ye cannot serve God and mammon." Does that mean that God will withhold mercy? No. God is good, better than I deserve, and I am blessed indeed that I am blessed; indeed, what He wills for my life is my salvation unto Him, and all prayers manifest to that end.

I once had a vision of just how much Jesus loves me. I saw myself sitting in my chair, in my home, in my neighborhood, in my state, in my country, on this world, all revolving around the sun's solar system, of God's universe, and it was apparent that none of these places would be affected by what I wanted or needed. I felt like an invisible speck. But! God saw me. He is affected by me. My griefs cause Him sadness, and He delights in my joy. This revelation caused me to be grateful for His care for me, a necessary mindset when asking Him for help.

I found that to live in this state of grace is not a daunting task as I finally figured out "my way or the highway" creates speed bumps, and the ride is smoother when I surrender the wheel and let God drive. In John 15:5, Jesus speaks, "I am the vine, ye are the branches: He that abides in me, and I in him, the same bringeth forth much fruit: for without me ye can do nothing." As I read this, a long, stashed memory came forward of having to call the bank about an overdraft charge.

I had made an error, and the bank charged me for it. I called requesting if the charge could be voided, and the clerk said, "No, you sound neither remorseful nor grateful enough that we covered the check at all." Flawed. She exhibited the grace of man. Thankfully, this is not how God's grace works.

One conceivable analogy would be when a child walks home after a tough day at school, knowing that in their backpack is a math test with a big red F on it. Their feet drag, their shoulders slump, their head is down, and their minds are busy with dread. But as they walk in the door, the smell of freshly baked chocolate chip cookies fills the air, the dog runs to greet them with tail wagging, and the parent looks at this child's face and smiles a big "Yay! You are home!" The child reluctantly pulls out the math test and hands it to the parent, who studies it intently and then sets it aside. The cookies are offered. And a chat ensues…

"Did you try my child?" "Yes."

"Is it too hard for you?" "Yes."

"Well, then let's get you some help. Have a cookie and go play? I will talk to them."

Our good God is humanly relatable in this. He is a loving, kind, patient gentleman who stands on manners and respects our free will to live with Him or not. He prefers that we see from our hearts and knows already what we need. Because God is love, love is His language. Everything He does is out of love. We should speak to Him from our hearts where our love exists. As long as we breathe, the love of God lives in our hearts. He is not bound by the constraints of time or our temperament.

## Secret Number 3 – Meet the Holy Spirit

"The Holy Spirit illuminates the minds of people, make us yearn for God, and takes spiritual truth and makes it understandable to us." Billy Graham.

I have been often asked how the Holy Spirit communicates with me. It is nothing like fairytales where we ride on moonbeams and are sprinkled with stardust. God is real. The Holy Spirit is real. And the communion with Him is real. I often see pictures in my thoughts and hear the image of words. When speaking in tongues, I am led on how to pray for others. He speaks to me through all my senses. I have seen Him, and He is barely five feet tall with wide-set almond-shaped eyes. I have smelled the fragrance of roses when praying for others. I have smelled His warmth. I have had the feeling of just "knowing." In discerning others, I have experienced the Holy Spirit "shakes" where the presence of God is overwhelming. This is usually accompanied by "get away from them" as an ego tries to trump Jesus or "Watch this! God is making a way."

When I paint, the ideas come from either a "bonk on the head" picture, a dream, a vision, a thought, or an idea that follows a recipe format. And just as they start, they end the same way. "It is done." Each piece is accompanied by scripture and quite often a song. This communing experience is a gift from the Holy Spirit as we create what He16nspirees me to do. Being of God, every piece carries a message of hope. They are of love and healing and become a roadmap back into God's grace.

To have this experience for yourself, invite Him into your life. To do so, follow Acts 2:38 to "repent, and be baptized in the name of Jesus Christ for the remission of sins, and ye shall receive the gift of the Holy Ghost," The Holy Spirit points all things to Jesus, and His primary source of information giving is the Bible. John the Baptist spoke in Matthew 3:11, "I indeed baptize you with water unto repentance, but He who is coming after me is mightier than I, whose sandals I am not worthy to carry. He will baptize you with the Holy Spirit and fire." Jesus. He also spoke of our need for the Holy Spirit, saying, "But the Helper, the Holy Spirit, whom the Father will send in My name, He will teach you all things, and bring to your remembrance all things that I said to you." John 14:16.

**Pray for Guidance**

Dear Jesus, I am amazed at the incredible love that has embraced me and all of the brokenness and alienation of the world around me. I love you, and I trust you. Take my life and shape me as you will. Open my eyes to the daily reality of your guidance through the Holy Spirit. And I am aware that my power cannot bring the transformation, change, or fruit you intend to bring. I invite you, Holy Spirit, to empower me. Take away my fears of what it means to submit my life to you. Take away my little expectations of what you can do through me. Open my eyes to needs and opportunities I have never seen before. Give me boldness in place of timidity. Exalt the name of Jesus in us and through me, and by your mighty, sovereign hand, move people toward Christ. In Jesus', Name. Amen.

Take time to get to know the Holy Spirit. He loves our lives, and He loves what God has made here. Once we are saved, He resides in our hearts, sealing us with the assurance of our soul's eternal state as He points our new thoughts and lives to all things Jesus. 2 Corinthians 4:16-18, our hope speaks of not losing heart as our inner self is being renewed day by day. And He comes with gifts from the Father.

Our Father loves to give gifts. But we are to look a gift horse in the mouth as the evil one tries to cheat us with cheap knockoffs. The false facades of the evil one, often in the guise of a spirit guide, can produce manifestations, including wondrous things, but they come with a catch, a payment due, of your immortal soul. Its gifts point all things to our earthly benefits or theirs and are short-lived.

Spirit guides are earth-bound spirits, demons that are an imposter of a benevolent being. Many will dog a family for generations, creating a facsimile of a generational curse. They get their information by eavesdropping or just playing the hunches knowing that the odds of 50/50 they might get it right. They will also become angry or flee if you test them according to 1 John 4 to test each spirit. I have seen them even mimic God's gift of the Word of Knowledge, which is the holy manifestation of the Father, via the Holy Spirit who points all things to Jesus.

## Trade Secrets of a Seer

The "Word of Knowledge" is defined as being given divine revelation from God, allowing us insight into certain situations. Unfortunately, and as is our nature to "fix and add" to what God freely gives, many look to the prophets and seers as God-approved psychics for a heads up requesting a Word of Knowledge to point the way out of their troubles, unknowing of the legitimacy.

How are we to know if imagination produced the statements or if they indeed were a message from Our Father? We will know when we apply thought and discernment to determine what is true or not...Does it cause the person to achieve a greater closeness to Jesus? Then, yes. Does it elevate the person into themselves and desires? Then, no. Do not rely on feelings, and do not gift, tithe, or pay in any way for it. God's Word is free! Apart from those specified in the Bible, all prophecy's success is determined by our cooperation as the parties involved have the free will to comply or not. Also, look to the life of those you seek knowledge from. Does their life reflect their walk with Jesus? Or is their inner "man" bleeding though and tainting the message?

I was once asked by someone who wanted to know what I thought about them having a spirit guide and even knowing its name. I replied, "He is an imposter. A demon has duped you into thinking it is a benevolent being. Use your intelligence and challenge it if you seriously want to know. They will do one of two things, depending on your relationship with Jesus. If it is lacking, they will become angry and pay you back for your insolence, or if your faith is strong, they will flee as you test them according to 1 John 4 "Beloved, do not believe every spirit, but test the spirits to see whether they are from God, for many false prophets have gone out into the world. 2 By this you know the Spirit of God: every spirit that confesses that Jesus Christ has come in the flesh is from God, 3 and every spirit that does not confess Jesus is not from God. This is the spirit of the antichrist, which you heard was coming and now is in the world."

My question is, "If your faith is strong in Jesus, why would you have a "spirit guide" in the first place? They are, after all, not the King of all heaven and earth. The Holy Spirit is."

And then there are the angels from heaven and their evil counterparts, demons. An angel is an emissary, or ambassador, with a mission or a message from God to you who will happily kneel at the name of Jesus as they worship Him with adoration. Like the good guys in the movies, they play by the rules while serving as heavens messengers and bodyguards. While understandable to be joyous in seeing them, be polite. Say thank you and keep your focus and worship on Jesus.

I have often seen them jump into a family pet to administer love where all other love is rejected, proving again that God does work in mysterious ways as His love always finds a way to us. And demons, being the bad guys, do not play by the rules, and their goal is to create chaos and havoc and destroy all that is good. Just because it is what they do.

As I said, the Holy Spirit points to Jesus, not the ego. Jesus said,

"Sheep won't follow a stranger; they will run from him because they don't know his voice." And John said in 10:5, "Yet they will by no means follow a stranger, but will flee from him, for they do not know the voice of strangers." As far as who do I listen to and acknowledge? The boss, the Holy Spirit, is the only one who can help. The rest? Mere peons who can only eavesdrop. When you "know," you "know."

Most of us learned reasonably quickly as children, that discreetly crossing our fingers behind our back means that we just told a lie, and it doesn't count in real life, much like stepping on a crack will break our mother's back. As adults, we must decide between the lie, the truth, and what is in between. The evil one attempts to manipulate segments of truth, as it did with Jesus in the desert. It is not the devil's folly to do this, for it is what it is. Our lesson is in how we answer it. Those employed by the devil are just as insidious, making it a good idea to claim Ephesians 6:10, "Finally, my brethren, be strong in the Lord and in the power of His might. 11 Put on the whole armor of God that you may be able to stand against the wiles of the devil."

Stand on the word of God, and just as the Declaration of Independence states, "We hold this self-evident to be true," in these end-of-days, it is imperative to fact-check all things against the Bible, for God is the only author of what is truth. Keep your balance in the Word.

Other's opinions can cause you to fall to monster bait. Stand on what is true, The Bible, and allow the Holy Spirit to confirm God's messages to you.

## Trade Secrets of a Seer

As we walk with God, we trust that things will turn out for the best as He is the only one who can thwart evil plans. The Holy Spirit urges us to make a move when the time is right, for our protection and safety. When we are in the holding pattern of waiting, rather than behave as in a forced timeout, use it as a time to spend quality time training with the Father.

My dad used to say, "Our first 100 years are the hardest." Well, ain't that the truth! He then shared that the hard days and hard people are not our end game but only a lesson, a purging, or even better, coming closer to Jesus' time. We are to stand on His word and walk in the faith of things unseen per 2 Corinthians 4:18, "So we fix our eyes not on what is seen, but on what is unseen, since what is seen is temporary, but what is unseen is eternal.

We must also step out of the hiding places we create and call to Him as the way maker of Isaiah 43, "See, I am doing a new thing! Now it springs up; do you not perceive it? I am making a way in the wilderness and streams in the wasteland." Make Jesus Lord of your days. Every day no matter what. No matter whom. Be a part of the victory because the evil one has staked his claim on this planet.

Consequently, incidences dodgeball all over our paths, causing fear, chaos, destruction, sadness, sickness, etc. And often, these experiences will be not just difficult but almost unbearable. Concentrate on the "almost" part. We are on His team; God always wins, and we have His Helper. As Christ prepared for his crucifixion to bear the burdens of my sins, he told his disciples in John 16, "for

He will take of what is Mine."

The Holy Spirit once told me the importance of being a "Halcyon." By saying "told," I mean that I have learned to know His voice as He speaks to me. It may be scriptural, audible, visions or dreams, signs, wonders, songs, poems, repetitions, or when my gaze is held for a split second longer than expected. This time, I had to search for what halcyon meant. I found that it is a bird much like a kingfisher that builds its nest in rough waters where it is safe. He then showed me Psalms 38, which tells me to rest in the Lord, without fretting, while He takes care of the problem. there will be a halcyon period in the latter days, where others find joy in strife. But those who focus on Jesus will have peace.

People have told me," Yeah, but you do not get it, Denise. I have been hurt! I have had trouble caused for no other reason than they were out to get me! I did not do anything to deserve it." Yes, I do get it. Lots of people get it. Woe songs are big business! A song that sings, "Nobody Knows the Trouble I've Seen, nobody knows my sorrow," has filled my thoughts more than a few dozen times. Words like loss, grief, despair, gloom, and doom seem to be the first place we all go when we think about our hurts. The question is, "Things that we are separated from Alex for $200, please" kind of thinking.

Separations are horrible! God knows! It is why He reminds us in Romans 8:38, "And I am convinced that nothing can ever separate us from God's love. Neither death nor life, neither angels nor demons, neither our fears for today nor our worries about tomorrow—not even the powers of hell can separate us from God's love. 39 No power in the sky above or in the earth below—indeed, nothing in all creation will ever be able to separate us from the love of God that is revealed in Christ Jesus our Lord." I count on it!

As we become more like Him, we will begin to mourn – ourselves, our human flaws. For a long time, when I thought I had the tiger by the tail, it bit me. When I realized I had done none of it on my own, for I am nothing without Him, I began to understand that my soul was impoverished, and it was only then that my soul began to soar. It could, as I finally got to quit waiting on my ego. Yes, a great ego is attached to our miseries. When we broadcast our woes and our "not fairs' rather than saying, "Thank you, Jesus, I know together will get through this, we establish to comfort ourselves by wrapping ourselves up in this new idol. When we learn to mourn, be saddened, and grief-stricken by our sin, we will find the heart of God, therefore, true happiness. As we step away from our wall, the Holy Spirit can get through to us to guide us in letting go of that which causes us pain. This, in turn, causes us to see Jesus, who can actually heal it.

The nudging's of the Holy Spirit will not leave and will not fade. No, not as when our attention refuses to budge on an idea, or even like an earworm, but as a neutral memory. Neither good. Nor bad. The thought is insistent but never compulsive.

For instance, I was in a store checking out, and the idea came to me to say to the clerk, "tell her she smells beautiful," popped into my mind as if it was a really, really great idea, so I did. And she smiled!

And then she said, "thank you! I was trying out a new perfume to see if it helped my long days here."

Another time, I was to gift a particular painting and was hesitant and procrastinating. The nudge came. I side-stepped it. Again, we went back and forth. I was trumped when the picture fell off the wall in front of me! Well, alrighty then! I packaged it right up and delivered it right then. How it was received is no longer my focus. That I was obedient to the Father was.

When the Holy Spirit nudges us to make a move or gives us a vision that we are to act upon, hours, days, weeks, in my case, once, years, sometimes will go by, and it will not fade like a dream. There will be no need to rush back to sleep to see if the shopping cart full of new shoes did make its way to you because, as it says in John 14:26, "But the Helper, the Holy Spirit, whom the Father will send in My name, He will teach you all things, and bring to your remembrance all things that I said to you." Put it out there regardless, just as God leads you.

God is my reality. I have never gone without once, and as long as I am His child, I never will. Psalms 52:8, "But I am like an olive tree flourishing in the house of God; I trust in God's unfailing love forever and ever." What is of God manifests these things per Galatians 5:22, "But the fruit of the Spirit is love, joy, peace, forbearance, kindness, goodness, faithfulness, 23 gentleness, and self-control. Against such things, there is no law. "

In our quest for the fruits and gifts of Spirit, it is human nature to tend to overlook that it is also His task to convict us of our sins. He does this so that when we are in God's presence in prayer or bask in His glory in praising Him, we stand as righteous as possible, for no one has the righteousness of Jesus on their own. The Holy Spirit will not work in a toxic environment. We must confess our sins and repent of them. Doing this allows us to be more sensitive to the spiritual things of God.

I cannot imagine any day without the Holy Spirit in it, and I understand why God is so incredibly protective of Him. In Mark 3, it says, "Assuredly, I say to you, all sins will be forgiven the sons of men, and whatever blasphemies they may utter; but he who blasphemes against the Holy Spirit never has forgiveness but is subject to eternal condemnation."

In a nutshell, the Holy Spirit is our counselor, at our invitation, helping us open our eyes, urging us into repentance, and pointing our walk to stay in alignment with Jesus. By God's grace, we can repent today of our sins. Thank Jesus, that God is merciful in our ignorance.

Clarifying the "yes buts" here… a person who commits intentional sin without repenting does not have the protective influence of the Holy Spirit, for He does not indwell with the unbeliever. What He does do is that He interacts with, influences, and affects unbelievers. Yay! Hope! However, disobedience to God's Word can suppress His activity in our lives. As we try and abide that the Holy Spirit is our counselor, at our invitation, helping us open our eyes, urging us into repentance, and pointing our path to getting in alignment with Jesus,

He will undoubtedly come through. Be co'forted, for no one born of God makes a practice of sinning on purpose.

It has been abundantly clear to me as the Holy Spirit continues to reveal why I was born and what my mission of love is. I am supposed to be here. It's not by chance, coincidence, or mistake, but by divine design. And my mission while I am here…to help others realize the same and, as we are all part of God's village, to see how much we are all wanted and needed by God. John 13:34, "A new command I give you: Love one another. As I have loved you, so you must love one another."

The best part of having daily conve'sations with the Spirit of Truth is that I no longer focus on me but on us as a whole. I have learned to no longer fear the sadness, for He has taught me fear that causes anxiety is the devil's domain, and that which I fear becomes a weapon it will use against me.

He also taught me that sadness is neither lethal nor contagious and that when I am sad, to recognize the cause, and often, it is only a temporary state. He taught me to stay away from the things that reflect back to me and look outward. To notice stuff. To see the scenarios that play out in others. Take a second look at those who stand behind the counters or on street corners. To stop and notice children playing. To listen to the sounds around me. To shut my eyes when I eat ice cream. To bury my face in a whole bouquet of roses just to inhale its fragrance. Do a crossword puzzle and just give my brain and heart a break. Why? All these things feed my soul, where He lives. And recognizing that God made this spectacular place with its stunning people and events welcomes my observations and participation. And to embrace that sooner than later, contentment will align itself with my new habits, and in contentment, happiness reigns. This is what a day in the life of the Holy Spirit is like.

I will live and not die. Ever. Why? Because I walk forward with Jesus in my heart and life, knowing I freely walking in with love beyond measure. It is easier to stay here because I have been baptized in the living waters of Jesus and the holy fire of the Holy Spirit, and I have literally stood in His glory.

## Invite The Holy Spirit Into Your Life

Oh, Holy Spirit, I have expectations about what I should and should not do. I now surrender to You my ideas, limitations, preferences, and goals. Fill me, Holy Spirit, with all Your supernatural gifts! Empower me to accept and grow in the supernatural life as the early disciples did. I want to be helpful to You. I want to go where You lead me. Holy Spirit, send me forth gifted and empowered to make a difference spreading the Good News of God's forgiving love.

Come, Holy Spirit; renew me. In Jesus' Name, Amen!

## Secret Number 4 – It is in How You Ask

Speak fitly. Fitly is defined as speaking in the proper manner or place or at the appropriate time. "A word fitly spoken is like apples of gold in pictures of silver." Proverbs 25:11.

Fitly

There are over 100 different Bible verses about the power of the human tongue. Psalm 141:3 "Set a guard, O Lord, over my mouth; keep watch over the door of my lips!" to Romans 10:9 "Because, if you confess with your mouth that Jesus is Lord and believe in your heart that God raised him from the dead, you will be saved." And in Matthew, the warning in 12:36, "I tell you, on the day of judgment people will give account for every careless word they speak." Yes, your words will come back to you sooner than later. Right here and right now, you will have as you say. Do your words bring life? Or do your words bring death?

Practice now that which you choose for yourself. Consider it studying up for the big final that will inevitably come. God will be reviewing them, and how they manifested will be noted. Did they harm? Or did they bring love? Make your words gold.

Talk to God. Ask Him how you are doing. I talk to God all the time. I ask Him questions, and He answers every one of them. Kindly. Patiently. Some come quickly, and some I have to wait on. He assures me that there are no wrong questions as I seek Him, and there's never been a time where He gave me the answer of "because I said so, and you shall not question me.

His patience is much appreciated as living among His children generates more questions. As He brings me into conversations with those with Jonah-type issues, those who sit in judgement of others and despise God's mercy upon those they deem unworthy of forgiveness, it is essential to ask questions! In our conversations with others, do they point us to seek Jesus' face? Or theirs? Do they uplift us to God, causing us to seek the answers in His word? Or do they say, "Because I said so and you shall not question me," which reeks of a tare, a "Christian" with a poisoning attitude.

Asking questions reveals our intent and puts us on the proper ground before God. James 1:5 states, "If any of you lacks wisdom, let him ask God, who gives generously to all without reproach, and it will be given to him."

Should I dare to approach my boss without an appointment, kick open the door demanding "get me more money right now," and think I will be successful is not something I, as a rational adult, with bills to pay, would do. I would be lucky to have a job after that. Most folks see the folly in that impatient 'I want what I want and right now' approach. It won't work with God either. Because our prayers take us into the presence of God, we are to first acknowledge Him. That He exists. We are to admit our unworthiness and ask forgiveness just as God said to Jeremiah to repent, to lose the attitude of despair and self-pity so that He can restore us to a state of inner peace. So then, when we stand before Him with our petitions, there are no walls, and we can bask in His love.

Through Christ and Christ alone, we have the right to approach God and ask for anything or to thank him for what He has provided. And the Amen? For so shall it be. So, when do you say, "Thank you, Jesus." In ALL things! Even in the hard things:

- Are you unhappy? Say, "Thank you, Jesus."
- Are "they" mean to you? Do "they" treat you poorly? Say, "Thank you, Jesus."
- Are you lonely? Say, "Thank you, Jesus."
- Are you ill or sick? Say, "Thank you, Jesus."
- Are you short of money? Say, "Thank you, Jesus."

- Are you concerned for another? Say, "Thank you, Jesus."
- Do you have too much to do? Say, "Thank you, Jesus."
- Are you depressed? Say, "Thank you, Jesus."

Implement this ideal. Why? Because God is love, and God works in love. A grateful heart is a manifestation of love. Is it easy to say this? No, not always. But say it anyway, even with gritted teeth if you must. Do not rely on your feelings. Rely on whatever faith you can muster. Why? Because it is biblical as well as the science behind cause and effect: That you get what you say whether it is good or bad, and whatever you spew, mutter, groan, mumble, grumble, speak, or state is what you can expect to boomerang back to you… and then some.

1 Thessalonians 5:18, "In everything give thanks; for this is God's will for you in Christ Jesus." This area is the devil's domain, and he is looking to take all that he can away from you, and he appreciates you specifying which thing has got you spun up. If you ask for more out of lack, you will most definitely get more lack. But! God knows our needs. He knows our path. He knows us. When we are ready to let go of what ails us, take a minute – but just a minute, lest we begin that path to woeful meandering again – and think about the present troubles. Then with a "thank you, Jesus, for this," give it to Him to take care of, for this is His domain and where He wants to shine all the blessings and healings and good stuff down upon you.

## Trade Secrets of a Seer

How does this work? By giving thanks, we open our hearts to gratitude. This will sound crazy but giving thanks for cancer, heart disease, diabetes, adultery, and so on, along with the rest of the issues our world offers, opens all of heaven to be put to work on your behalf while it slams the door shut on the devils harassing you. So when you say, "Thank you, Jesus, for these troubles," rest assured Jesus will most definitely answer you with, "you are welcome! I got it from here. It is not to trouble you again." It is true. Try it. Oh, and by the way… if it does, give it back to Him. As humans, we are notorious for playing out the game of "No, that is okay, I can handle it now" and taking things back under our control.

Your words have the power to heal or harm… yourself! When you speak, "I can and will go wherever and whenever Jesus wants me to go," well, then get your passport up to date as you just loosed all of heaven to be your travel agent.

I have also observed an uptick in warnings to heed "things are looking bad, so we better stock up on everything." Well, yes, now it is, and yes, now you better as the devil is laying claim to this world with your words keep him there, you just permitted him to rob you. So go ahead and stock up and expect it to spoil long before you can use it, for this is how the devil plays this game. Instead of speaking the devil into more work for you, try it this way:

"My God provides for me faithfully. I have everything I need." Stock up as God leads you, but not through fear.

I need to include the all too common "pray for me as I am sick "… why yes, now you are, and should you choose to get sicker, keep talking like this. The devil may toy with you and let – yes, let – you get better for the moment, as he has more illness waiting for you to speak into existence.

Of course, we are to pray for each other! But watch your words should you bind another with them. Ask for prayer with hope and faith, expecting God to hear, knowing that God will provide. Ask expectantly, "Please pray for me. This situation I have here is not of God, and I do not want it in my life. Jesus and I have things to do, and I need to be on my A-game to give Him my best. I need His anointing" just as when Jesus' half-brother James wrote, "Is anyone among you sick? Let them call the elders of the church to pray over them and anoint them with oil in the name of the Lord." James 5:14

The focus was the anointing in the confidence of healing, not the illness. Return to God that which is God's, meaning you, and call upon the Name of Jesus to bring Him back into your life and into your prayers. Go forward loving and live accordingly. The Lord says, "Call upon me in the day of trouble. As promised in Joel 2:42, Acts 2:21, and Romans 10:13, "Everyone who calls on the Name of the Lord will be saved. Through prayer, invite Jesus into your heart to become your personal Lord and Savior.

For me... God answers all my prayers because the Holy Spirit often shares what the needs are to pray for and how God desires to hear about them. Always ending with Your will be done, Father, In Jesus' Name. Amen.

"God gives me whatever I want because I want whatever He gives."
Author Unknown

## Secret Number 5 – Faith over Fear

"Chapter one: The night was humid." No, this is not Chapter one but Secret Number 5, and the morning was hot. And moist. It was the dog days of the summer of 2018.

There is a story in the Book of Mark of an ill child who was presumed dead by the local synagogue leader who suggested to the crowd not to bother Jesus with the dead, as the authority of Jesus was a prominent thorn in his side. The people asked Jesus to go anyway; as He approached this "dead" child, He said, "Little girl, I say to you, get up." And she did! Alive and well and hungry!

This parable sets the stage for a story about my husband, who called to say he had had a tough night resting after the long workday had wrapped up late, as expected, leaving a bite to eat at the local bar. He ordered up, spiced it up, slammed it down, and beat it back to the RV camper to rest. His restful sleep was subverted by hours of painful coughing. Being him, the love of my life was determined to "walk it off" and still went to work at sunrise. I was concerned but not alarmed, as this was our "normal." He is, after all, a bridge rebuilder. He was raised to work hard, provide for his family, and suck it up. Days later, as symptoms set in, he reluctantly saw a doctor, who was also unconcerned. But my Holy Spirit's "spide-y senses" were tingling, and worries invaded my thoughts. I felt fear. I know fear is a liar, but it pushed hard to take hold, so I gave it to Jesus. Who in turn gave me Romans 5:5, "And hope maketh not ashamed; because the love of God is shed abroad in our hearts by the Holy Ghost which is given unto us," emphasizing the joy of all the hellos my husband and I have had. He also gave me a vision of my husband. Yes, God felt my worry, and in compassion, He granted a vision of my mate walking out of the pole barn as a very old and happy man. I smiled a big "thank you, Jesus, I trust you." This vision spurred my faith as I wiped away the tears to put on my battle gear attitude. The devil knows when the tears stop, it is his "uh-oh she's awake" notice as I claim the war cry "Greater is He, i.e., God, in me than he, i.e., the devil, is in this world" heralded in John 4:4 The devil just lost the battle in the spiritual realm. I still called in for backup and asked a friend to pray for us. We thanked God for His mercy, and as we claimed the Resurrection Prayer, he received a Word of Knowledge for me to "not believe the lies." My faith said that God was in control.

I waited a long time to find this man, and in the end, he found me. And we live our faith in the most basic of God's principles of "you get what you say." We apply God's Book of motivational speeches, Proverbs, in particular Proverbs 18:21, "Death and life are in the power of the tongue: and they that love it shall eat the fruit thereof." This stems from Isaiah 55:11, "So shall my word be that goeth forth out of my mouth: it shall not return unto me void, but it shall accomplish that which I please, and it shall prosper in the thing whereto I sent it."

And with the need to see how our beloved was, our granddaughters, Angel and Sugar, drove with me to see Papa for ourselves. We were still four hours away when he called to say he met with another doctor, a reticent man, who diagnosed him with pneumonia caused by aspiration but expected a full recovery. Thank you, Jesus! We finally arrived at the camper, happy to see his face, with hugs and tears, accompanied by the "you scared me's!" He was exhausted and lay down. A few hours later, he awoke, and his breathing was erratic. I called this new doctor, who asked us to meet him at the local emergency room. We arrived, checked in, and were sent to a small room where the nurses took his vitals and helped him onto the gurney along with our six-year-old granddaughter, Angel, insisted she get to cuddle her Papa to help him feel better.

The resident doctor came in and wrote his name on the whiteboard. He ordered tests and said he would be back after reviewing the results. He eventually came back accompanied by "the look" and "the news" that the tests were concerning to him, and the admitting doctor would be in to talk with us. He erased his name and left. I said out loud, "I trust you, Jesus." And then dun-dun-dunnnn… all hell broke loose!! An imposing figure of a man entered, who wrote his name on the whiteboard. He turned and faced me across my husband on the gurney and elaborated on the test results. He decided for us an immediate admission to the oncology department. I was shocked! This was so wrong! Oh! Wait a minute! Wait a minute! Wait just a minute! And a spiritual war started right there, in full sight of the hospital staff, our granddaughters, and anyone else in earshot. I countered his "diagnosis" with the greater authority of Jesus. His diagnosis was a lie. I spoke, "My husband has pneumonia. He does not need oncology treatment. He only aspirated into his lungs. The only thing that is wrong with him is that he eats stupid when he is not home."

He retorted, "Ma'am, please contact your family as you need help. You are being foolish and unreasonable." Unfazed, I said, "I will. They will back me up. We prayed God would make this right. I repeat, my husband has pneumonia. And it will be healed." Leaving the room, he looked back and said, "Ma'am, you need help." I replied, "I have help. I have Jesus." He replied, "Good luck with your little religion." With head shaking, he left to write up the admitting papers. As I watched him go, I said, "I trust you, Jesus." My heart pounded, and I felt ill. I looked at my mate and asked him if he could wake up enough to watch the girls as I needed to go and collect myself. As always, he smiled, "Of course, I will."

I opened the door and stepped out into the corridor of the twilight zone. I was enveloped in a sea of orange jumpsuits on prisoners, surrounded by armed guards, brought in chain-gang style for medical care, which added to the surreality of the situation. I stepped to the side and kept my back against our door, thinking, "Lord, I need my people." The face of a beloved friend popped into my thoughts, and I called him. He listened and advised me, "No way would any good doctor ever give a diagnosis like that and certainly not under those conditions! Hold your own!" I hung up the phone, and my son-in-law's face then popped in as well. I called him. As soon as I heard his voice, the stress broke, and I cried.

He 'sked, "Where are you?" I told him the story so far.

He asked, "Are the girls a problem? I can come and get them."

I replied, "No."

He said, "Is Papa okay?"

I said, "He will be."

He then said, "No way would any good doctor ever give a diagnosis like that and certainly not under those conditions! Hold your own!"

I hung up and walked back to the room. The nurse side-eyed me and said quietly, "If you like, you can tell me to erase the doctor's name from the whiteboard." I told her, "Do it." She left to notify him that his services were no longer wanted. God, please bless her! At long last, and the angels sang when in walks our doctor! He softly spoke, "What is going on here? What are they saying to you?"

Although he already knew, he listened and shook his head, "Oh no! no! He has no cancer! He is fine. It is only pneumonia, and all will be fine. We will admit him for further observation, but yes, he is fine. We will send him upstairs and take good care of him. Do not worry." They wheeled the gurney with my beloveds to his room, treated him for pleurisy, and prescribed rest, medication, and instructions to eat more sensibly before bed. All was well. Peace was back in the realm.

As I look back, I think, "But by the grace of God, it could have gone a whole lot differently. How do people believe the lies and get through these things without Jesus to fight it for them?" This is one more benchmark that God is our authority, and we are to exercise our rights as His children. Isaiah 53:5 states very clearly, "But he was wounded for our transgressions, he was bruised for our iniquities: the chastisement of our peace was upon him, and with his stripes, we are healed." Thank you, Jesus, for your mercies.

In summary, was God negating the medical profession? No. Was God negating this doctor? No. Mark tells the story of Jesus' thoughts on "Paying the Imperial Tax to Caesar," where authority figures challenged Jesus on His opinion of Man's laws vs. God's laws regarding paying taxes to the government. Jesus asked the authorities to bring Him a coin. They did. He then asked them to look at it and tell Him whose image was on it. They replied, "Caesar's." And Jesus answered and said to them, "Render to Caesar the things that are Caesar's, and to God the things that are God's." Mark 12:17.

In this medical experience, I could not allow my faith to be coerced into admitting a lie to be true. Instead, I put evil on notice when I spoke the truth. Was it easy? No. But I still spoke.

Because God is a God of order, not chaos, we must teach ourselves to respond vs. reacting logically. This was my "moo" time to see from God's perspective. The applicable logic in my husband's health situation vs. the doctor's opinion is not that he was lying but he based his views on a vague image. Oncology was neither his field of expertise nor did he run the specific tests to back up his opinion. His presumed authority was being used as a "hitman" by evil to get me to speak the lie, which then would allow it to become a reality at some point. If not now, then later.

Does this mean that those who have, or are, or could possibly be ravaged by cancer be out of God's will? Absolutely not! I have a most beautiful and wonderful friend who was diagnosed and did have to have surgery, even though we prayed. As we prayed, I heard, "I am sorry, my blessed child, that this cup is before you. I will be with you and not leave you. I will not forsake you. You will live and not die. You are a blessing to me and to others. I will make this up to you." And I see her as flawless, just as God does. Why this mountain was placed before her to cross is unknown to me. I know she is a blessing to many, and maybe God needed her there for someone else who needed to see her faith in action. God has His plans. We are to thank Him in the storms and find peace within them. We later met for lunch and a cute little diner with red and white booths. And it hit me out of the blue, and I spoke, "By His stripes, you were healed." Yes, were. And yes again, He did make it up to her—an all-expense-paid beach vacation and more years to her life.

The prayer we prayed claims the power that resurrected Jesus Christ out of death, opened the tomb, and transfigured Him into heaven, and we as His children have full access to it. It calls on Ezekiel 37:4, "Again he said unto me, Prophesy upon these bones, and say unto them, O ye dry bones, hear the word of the Lord. 5 Thus saith the Lord God unto these bones; Behold, I will cause breath to enter into you, and ye shall live" Call forth the resurrection power that lays within us by the power of Jesus Christ to come forth knowing every believer in Jesus Christ has a seed within them that will raise a dead body to life or transform a body into a glorified one.

When we speak the Bible out loud, along with our prayers, God honors His word "that no spoken word ever returns void," and the devil hears them as well! He now knows that God will set loose all of heaven to fight on our behalf and that he already lost. But like most fighters that cheat to win, the devil will throw in a few zingers to rattle us into conceding to the loss just by wishing to make it all stop and go away. For me, in this time, he threw in the fear factor of bloodied up prisoners and guards with guns to make the whole thing a nightmare that I only wanted to wake from rather than fight through. They were just a rented supporting cast that he used.

As I said, my dear husband, Duane, works rebuilding bridges. One of the specialty trucks he uses extends a basket up, out, and over the side of the bridge and then down below it and holding a two-man crew underneath it is suspending them high over a river or a concrete highway to fix its expansion joints. Their bravery boggles my mind.

I rode along with him one Sunday afternoon as he checked on the recently poured concrete. And the bridge moved. It moved a lot! It moved with every big passing truck, and I also noticed it was a LONNNGGG WAY DOWN to the river below. He looked at my distress and said, all too familiar, "Babe, it is fine. You are okay. It is really good that it does that. As long as it keeps moving, the bridge is well. It is when it stops moving that it is not good." (I love it when he takes that tone with me.) "Oh duh!" I thought, and common sense aligned with physics took hold of my thoughts. Every bridge deck rests on pillars designed to carry the load through the water to the footings below on a solid foundation. And at this, the Holy Spirit piqued my interest so He could show me the comparison.

Bridges, like people, are designed to flex. Rigidity, both in people and structures, is a disaster in the making and will fail at the most inopportune time. Duane had once worked a bridge a few days before it collapsed. It had lost its flex and became rigid, causing a catastrophic accident. He lost friends. The point of this comparison shown was to be as a parable. The Bible lists seven wisdom pillars; fear of the Lord, instruction, knowledge, understanding, discretion, counsel, and reproof. We need to rest on these. We are to implement these to fight to be free in Jesus. Many jump on the reproof to distract from our sins is to point out those in others. But I digress… When we allow fear to override our faith or become anchored in an ideal or opinion, we become rigid and lock heaven out. God cannot use unyielding people and will replace them with those willing to serve and be a blessing.

In Matthew 22:36, "Master, which is the great commandment in the law? 37 Jesus said unto him, thou shalt love the Lord thy God with all thy heart, and with all thy soul, and with all thy mind. 38 This is the first and great commandment. 39 And the second is like unto it. Thou shalt love thy neighbor as thyself. 40 On these two commandments hang all the law and the prophets." There are no addendums, no amendments, no "yes but's." These two commandments are our expansion joints. They rest on the pillars that sink deep through the waters, the mud, the mire, the opinions swirling around them and stand on our rock. Jesus.

For instance, if everyone agreed on everything, well, first, that'd be boring, and second, how would we grow in Him? Jesus paid the price for us. We need to pay it forward by keeping His commandments in Matthew. If we are genuinely in Christ, that is our job. Whoever God puts on your path… love them as Jesus loves them. Whatever mountain casts a shadow upon you, climb it with Jesus. Our path in Jesus is the flexing expansion joints. He is our pillar. Our words and actions are the bridge. Keep the faith, baby!

## The Resurrection Prayer

Dear Jesus,

Help me understand that your life, death, and resurrection was not in vain.

Every time a negative thought begins to form in my mind,

help me instead be grateful that you suffered unbearably,

just for me. That you suffered so that I did not have to means

I can give all my worries and cares to you while at the same time

moving forward because of your resurrection power

that brings dead things to life.

In Jesus' Name. Amen

Trade Secrets of a Seer

**Ask for God's Anointing**

Father God,

I anoint this body, and I claim your resurrection power on

this day to cover my mind, body, and soul, my health,

my finances, my family, my friends,

all areas of our lives in Jesus' name.

I understand that by claiming your resurrection

power for my life daily,

I am joyful, in Jesus' name.

I have all my needs met in Jesus' name.

I am healthy, in Jesus' name.

I am made whole.

In Jesus' Name. Amen

## Secret Number 6 - Loopholes & Opinions

There is a parable in Luke of the kind of thing the devil does to utilize any loopholes. It is called the Parable of the Empty House. Luke 11:24, "When the unclean spirit is gone out of a man, he walketh through dry places, seeking rest; and finding none, he saith, I will return unto my house whence I came out."

We had hung a plaque in our home that read, "Forever, For Always, and No Matter What." Then the weird uptick in arguments started. Even though no ill intentions were involved, we consented to the "no matter what" with the action incurred by hanging it up. Together, we asked the father to intercede and show us a way out of the arising pettiness and to bless our home and us. We then realized that we agreed to imply consent to "the no matter what" part.

Innocuous enough, this "no matter what" leaves a murkiness, i.e., "I will love you, no matter what — even if" is a loophole.

Picky?

Absolutely!

The stakes for our immortal soul are very high. It says in Ephesians 6:12, "For we wrestle not against flesh and blood, but against principalities, against powers, against the rulers of the darkness of this world, against spiritual wickedness in high places." To live in the power of Jesus, we must rebuke all things that are not of Him. For if they are not of God, then they are of evil. There is no middle ground. This applies to objects, people, and places. So again, we prayed, "To this we rebuke, we cancel, and we call on Jesus to destroy every assignment and attack of the enemy being used against us and cancel every curse or negative word ever spoken over our lives. In Jesus' Name. Amen."

So, what to do, what to do? Well, we need to shut the door!

How?

The Bible says in Romans 12:21, "Be not overcome of evil, but overcome evil with good." All good comes from God, and He has sent us the Holy Spirit to counsel us to live like Christ. And we prayed, "Father, thank you for our salvation in Jesus. We ask by the blood of Jesus who washed this void, now clean of sin, strengthen it by your spirit in Jesus' name. Holy Spirit, please come, fill, and seal this vacancy afresh in your power. In Jesus' Name. Amen.

Even my own mother, an avid card player, hoped to gain the rewards of implied consent and often said, "I think God gave me three girls to always play my favorite card game of Bridge with me anytime. Much to her dismay, this middle child of hers had no interest in any card games. Was her assumption that this was why she had three girls correct? Maybe. Maybe not.

We tend to assume that our opinions are correct. We tend to assume that the Bible will follow along with our knowledge of things. We tend to assume that most everything is about us; the good, the bad and the ugly. We tend to assume that our feelings are factual and "if it feels good" then do it. A lot of sin tends to feel good... at first. And "if it feels bad" then don't do it, such as getting up and going to work on the day after the big game. God never told us to trust our feelings. He told us to trust His Word for it never fails and it never lies. So before you just assume something is good and right and feels good and right, double check it against the Holy Spirit residing within you.

I have come upon many who offer opinioned prophecies. Some are legit. Some should just quit. An easy check is this; is it what you want to hear? That's rarely God. Lol! Is it going to require a pretty drastic rethinking of your ideas and send you to floor on your knees to Jesus? That's probably God.

What trips up many a reasonable person of God are assumptions. Other than biblical prophecies, all other words, consents, dreams, visions, etc., usually require our cooperation. So before you buy the house, buy the wedding dress, or make any decisions based on what someone said they heard from God, double-check it! Does it hold up with the Bible verse 2 Corinthians 10:5, "Casting down imaginations, and every high thing that exalteth itself against the knowledge of God, and bringing into captivity every thought to the obedience of Christ?" Before making any move, consider getting on your knees before God and searching for His will on your path, just as the Psalms read.

"Yeah, but they said… and the excuses ramp up." I once dreamed of a mouse inside a bag of raisins belonging to someone I knew. I noticed they had been eating out of it.

Well, first… ewww. And secondly, the Holy Spirit alerted me that the mouse stood for cowardice and jealousy. The bag was the power play. What struck me was that the raisins were dried-up fruits, no longer symbolizing gratitude of one's attitude. All I will elaborate on is that it isn't pleasing to God to pray for someone else to be getting a speeding ticket because they made you mad. You might find yourself getting one…

The Bible is based 100% on our restoration to God and counsels us in Proverbs 12:5 to be wise when we seek the advice of others, saying, "The thoughts of the righteous are just, But the counsels of the wicked are deceitful." Proverbs 12:15 even warns, "The way of a fool is right in his own eyes, But a wise man is he who listens to counsel." This means you need to consider what lies in the plan or ego of the one advising you. The doctor was advising us, but his own agenda and ego clouded the truth. Always take it straight to Jesus. His word and love are freely given, for He is the lover of our souls, the only one who sincerely has our best interest at heart.

Even as a seer praying for another receives knowledge in a vision, they should clarify it with the Holy Spirit before sharing it. Giving another what is seen is not always the answer. Occasionally, a seer is shown only to enhance the prayer time in the right direction as the Holy Spirit prefers to see an effort on their part to establish a working relationship with Him. He conveys God's wishes best when we read the Bible ourselves. Malachi 2:7 reads,

"For the lips of a priest should preserve knowledge, and men should seek instruction from his mouth; for he is the messenger of the Lord of hosts." We must speak as a messenger of our Lord. It is written "God said," not Bob or Carol or Ted or Alice said. Or even as

Denise said. Ask Him to confirm the counsel you receive from others. He showed me again the lurking mouse dream. And still…ewww.

When Jesus was tempted by the devil in the desert, the trial He was in was how He would respond to the temptations thrown at Him. Jesus recognized that the devil was just doing his job to torment and torture and that the lesson was His.

How did Jesus deal with these troubles and temptations?

He said no.

One morning, I reaped a lesson in heeding the Holy Spirit! As soon as my eyes opened from a great sleep, my mind was bombarded with the "must do now's!" The laundry was calling, the dog needed his allergy medicine, the dishwasher wanted unloading, the five-year-old fridge was on the blink, and the food needed to be dealt with, which was just the first page of the mental list.

I got up. I heard the Holy Spirit say, "Read My word." I said "Okay" and checked the laundry. I heard Him say again, "Read My word." I said, "Okay" as I gave the pills to the dog and let him outside. Again, I heard "read My word." I said, "I will." as I unloaded the dishwasher. And yet again, I heard, "Read My word." Now I am a little annoyed, and I say, "Father, the thing about Mary and Martha is that there were two of them," and again, I heard "Read My word" without any annoyance in the tone. Tea is now made. The dryer is drying. The dog is back in. The dishwasher is emptied. The floors are mopped up, and I finally get to sit down in my chair to read His word, to start my day right.

I kid you not, the day's meditation started with "Cause me to hear thy loving kindness in the morning; for in thee do I trust: cause me to know the way wherein I should walk; for I lift up my soul unto thee.

Psalms 143:8 Followed by "Come unto me, all ye that labour and are heavy laden, and I will give you rest." Matthew 11:28. And not one "I told you so... "but a sense of peace in its stead. Let's just say that the lesson is learned again. Father, forgive me for my annoyance and my idols made up of poor priorities. God comes before all, just like it says in Matthew 6:33, "But seek ye first the kingdom of God, and his righteousness and all these things shall be added unto you."

The First Commandment is "You shall have no gods before Me."
Can you imagine putting the needs of the dishwasher before your spouse or your boss, asking for a friend?

## Secret Number 7 - The Spiritual Realm

Joel prophesied of a future time, before Jesus Christ's return when there would be heavenly signs and "your old men shall dream dreams, your young men shall see visions" Joel 2:28-31. The apostle Peter used this prophecy to help explain the extraordinary miracles that accompanied the giving of God's Spirit on the Day of Pentecost in Acts 2:15- 17.

Speaking with authority in Jesus became a learned behavior for me. I was born with a preference for being set apart to recreate what is in my thoughts. Okay then, a wallflower. I figured God had enough people taking care of enough people that I could just paint my life through, but He had other ideas. Relinquishing the scenic route years later and now living what I was born to be, I paint and write for Jesus Christ, Son of God, Lord of lords, and King of kings. My inspiration comes from the Holy Spirit intentionally through dreams and visions. The more I read my Bible, the more I understand the images He gives. These dreams are as clear the next day, as the next month, or even thirty years later as they are as bright and clear as the day, I dreamed them. The visions given are as a wide-awake dream or something that holds my gaze for that odd split second longer as my mind registers it. I always ask for His guidance as I draw scripture into my paintings. Because I have seen the dark side, it can be no other way. I am at one with God. I have a seat at His table, and He has a seat at mine.

It has been said, "The more you know, the more you know," and as a Christian, the more you believe, the more you believe. And the more you believe, the more God moves. This is a great segue into sharing my experience of The Veil.

In the summer of 2020, at just past 11 pm, I had awakened to a real-life "I can see this vision as plain as day" of white linen, almost gauzy, fabric floating over me on my bed, a foot below the ceiling. Yes, I was awake! I sat up to kneel on the bed just as it dropped down upon my head. This act caused me to flinch as it "hit" my head. There was no physical impact as it touched me, but instead, it absorbed into my body, and I felt a new anointing from Jesus. I just experienced real life Ephesians 1:17, "That the God of our Lord Jesus Christ, the Father of glory, may give unto you the spirit of wisdom and revelation in the knowledge of him:" This anointing was personal, and I felt like a "knowing" was gifted unto me. According to the Psalms, the invitation to willingly kneel before God, the Great Creator, not out of protest but in need to be truly loved. I am loved. I have no doubt.

It wasn't long after the veil experience that I was having a particularly hard day and checked in to bed early. As I lay there, I said my prayers and praised God for my blessings, and I could hear my gram's voice in my memory singing Count Your Blessings, name them one by one; Count your blessings, see what God hath done; Count your blessings, name them one by one; Count your many blessings. See what God hath done." And the room began to sparkle as the Glory Cloud of God descended upon me. As I knelt on the bed, I was enveloped in a slow, swirling whirlwind of golden flecks, and love was indeed in the air. I raised my arms, and I cried, for I had never been so homesick to just go home. Zechariah 2:5 became my reality, "For I declare the Lord will be a wall of fire around her, and I will be the glory in her midst." And then it left. And I had been made well of a chronic neck pain that had plagued me for two years. I had gone to physical therapy. I had gone to chiropractors. I had been to medical doctors who were trying to help me yet relying on pharmacia, while others had recommended fusion surgery.

I said no even when the pain had pushed me to bed. Each and every time, I cried out "thank you Jesus for this. I praise you Jesus for this. And by the way Jesus, I cannot paint for you in bed so please heal me." I never once complained about my lot. I never once doubted my God. And in this time, I experienced His ministering love as He sent an angel into my dog to come and sit by me when I could hardly bear it.

Yes, our beloved pets, who never got themselves banished from Paradise, are vessels for the Father to send an extra dose of love when needed. Yes, in that instance, I was healed. The experience was worth the wait.

Everything about God is so supernatural that He is dismayed when He, as the boss of all supernatural realities, sees us dabbling with the new age, cults, psychics, mediums, ghostbusters, demon servants, etc.

Even in Leviticus 19:31 says, "Regard not them that have familiar spirits, neither seek after wizards, to be defiled by them: I am the Lord your God." You will serve the evil one by default if you do not serve God.

## Trade Secrets of a Seer

Since my earliest memory at age 4 of the elderly man who "lived" in my childhood home, I have seen the supernatural and spirits. He was quiet and bothered no one, but he left an aura of depressed feelings. We loved the neighborhood, but it was a neighborhood of tragedies. One little boy was killed in a house fire, another baby boy died of SIDS, another little boy died from inhaling parts of a burst balloon, the son next door was crushed by his car, a dad drowned while fishing leaving behind a very angry son, and my own brother began his adventures in drug abuse. We eventually moved away, and my parents began hosting Bible studies, and we all became "born again Christians" and were filled with the Holy Ghost.

Before I knew better, I would consult mediums in foolishness rather than total ignorance, as I lost my people to tragedies. I assumed God would allow the good ones, like angels, to help me find closure, and it made me the perfect patsy. In this foolish quest, I learned the devil counterfeits everything God does but aims for our destruction instead of our peace. Because the Intuitive's were very intuitive and provided easy-to-believe information, I figured it had to be legit. Right? Wrong! The Holy Spirit began convicting me of this folly, so I finally asked God about it. I accepted the Holy Spirit's counsel in this quest, and the more reality of it I saw, the more I complied with God's Word. And the more I complied with Him, the more of the insidiousness trap I saw. These things prey upon the desperate.

One afternoon, I treated myself to a television time-out. As I channel surfed, I came across a psychic medium show. I was going to keep scrolling when the Holy Spirit said, "Watch this." Okay? I stopped. Now in the hot seat, He showed me the familiar spirit, a polite term for a demon, that this intuitive was talking with. The thing was imitating the deceased father and relaying personality traits and mannerisms just as the dead dad did. It was all just a show! And they were literally playing with a demon on a demonic assignment which meant no good. These spirits will follow a family's bloodline for generations with the intent to instigate death and destruction. They are masters of the facade, and it is critical to know what we are inviting into our home and heart per Leviticus 10:10, "And that ye may put difference between holy and unholy, and between unclean and clean;" And I swear the devils have a quota.

Shortly after this, and out of the blue, a "friend" sent me a video regarding their concern about a witch colony and wished for me to pray for them. As soon as I saw the attachment, I started feeling skittish, and inside me, I heard a "No!" from the Holy Spirit! They defended that they were asking me to watch it so we could have an in-depth conversation about how to pray. Again, I got a "No!" from the Holy Spirit. I told the person, "This is not to be on my plate," and then the cajoling ramped up as to why we should and that I should give it a chance and go ahead and just watch it. Delete. Delete. Delete. God does not plead, and I laid it at the cross.

Later that day, the Holy Spirit suggested we talk about it. Welllll… He spoke, and I listened. I got the feeling that this was going to be a big lesson. He then showed me when this good Christian person opened the video and watched it, a familiar spirit was released, counting on the premise that the viewer cannot unsee what was seen or un-hear what was heard, thus giving it a foothold on you. He asked me to call a prayer warrior friend, and sure enough, this whole scenario was textbook Jezebel, a hideous demon known to argue, cajole, threaten, plead, beg, etc., often all simultaneously. There is one devil, but he has a crew of many spirits that belong to this category. Yes, they are cliques in hell.

This queen bee specialty squad of hitmen is named after a prophet killer called Queen Jezebel from the days of the Prophet Elijah. In this case, the devil was on a deliberate witch hunt.

To nullify all of this evil, I needed to speak out loud," I rebuke this attack. I plead the shed blood of Jesus over myself from this conversation, and no more will any demon talk to me. I have no interest in the devil or what it is doing, only in Jesus. I have no interest in witches or what they are doing. I am neither enthralled nor repelled by them as my God is greater." I placed the demon on notice. You bring in one bad apple, and the fruit flies are all over the rest of them.

Did you know that when you call out a demon or the more congenial term of familiar spirit, they get loud! And they shriek! Even in a text. Ick!

I have seen the devil. I have seen demons. I have seen them in the supernatural and I have seen them in people. As a seer, stop doubting what you are being shown. You... know. I have heard the lies. I have no time or patience for them.

My thoughts, as my life, are on Jesus only.

Familiar spirits mimic the love feels, but it is neither real nor lasting and will leave one with greater emptiness leaving the broken bits of the heart to gape even wider, creating a false need to go back for more and more. This plan, which by the way, pays their bills, is the basis of all predators. To take from you and that is not love and certainly not God's kind of love.

When God loves, it envelops and fills all the cracks, and God's angels will not deliberately call attention to themselves. They direct all things, all glory, all worship, to Jesus. And when God heals, it is once and done per "by whose stripes you were healed." You WERE. Once and done! Believe it! With the lesson clarified, the Holy Spirit pointedly asked, "Why to settle for lies and half-truths when Jesus is the truth?" and I said, "Lord, you made your point. Forgive me." Now for clarification about this once and done... healing is a process which includes acceptance. With Jesus, you were. But from the human perspective healing can take a lifetime and is a process and it's okay, Jesus is with you each step of the way. In James 5:15 it says, "And the prayer of faith will save the sick, and the Lord will raise him up. And if he has committed sins, he will be forgiven. James does not say the sick will always be raised up instantly. Just that they will be raised. "They will recover."

Oh yes, angels are so very real. I was once asked if I had ever seen an angel and if I was afraid of it? Yes, I have often seen them, and no, there is no fear in anything that comes from God. And I trust them to do their job.

Early one morning, I stepped off the commuter bus onto the still darkened street and walked quickly in the cold to my building. I saw the secured elevators were out of service, leaving me no choice but to take my ride up in the freight lift. I no more had stepped in when around the corner came a raggedy-looking man about to join me on my solo ride.

But he stopped short! His eyes went straight up behind me, and he said, "uhh, I think I will wait," and did a quick about-face and left. As I turned to see what he was looking at, I caught a glimpse of my large and in-charge guardian angel dressed in his usual brown monk garb, the attire of one of God's worker bees as in Psalms 91:11 "For he shall give his angels charge over thee, to keep thee in all thy ways." Yes, God will instruct His angels to watch over us as His angel's purpose is to guard His children.

Those who are faithful will be under the constant care of His angels and occasionally be redirected back onto the path of righteousness. And as the lessons are sometimes tantalizing, they do get their point across. And as His messengers, they prompt us as well to do the right thing at the right time.

I had just had a good and long impromptu talk with my big sister on the phone. The next day she died. The second day after, I saw her appear in my apartment's hallway. I was perplexed if this was really her. I questioned it. After all, I knew it was like a demon to portray a loved one. But God showed me when Apostle Peter referred to Jesus going to preach to those "imprisoned spirits" in 1 Peter 3:18, "For Christ also hath once suffered for sins, the just for the unjust, that he might bring us to God, being put to death in the flesh, but quickened by the Spirit" through to verse 22, "Who is gone into heaven, and is on the right hand of God; angels and authorities and powers being made subject unto him."

I asked her where she was, and she shrugged her shoulders "and said, right now? I am neither here nor there." But then, excitedly, she said, "Wait till you hear what I will be doing!" I asked, "What?" She said, "I will be taking care of the babies." She will be great at it her new job. She was a great auntie. She was 27 years old. Mom and dad were in the car with her. Mom went through the windshield and still applied successful CPR to her while praying fervently. But in the end, the distracted driver ended her life. They drew closer to God.

My dad had his first heart attack in his early fifties. And lived through many, many more for the next 20 years. Every visit and phone call was met with the thought that this was the last time. The weight of it was impalpable. Although it was a fantastic experience to see the growth of cardiology from sandbagging his chest and weeks of being bedridden to out of the surgery and out the door in hours, the experiences took their toll on our family. He was only 72 when he went home, but I was yet not done being a daddy's girl. It is a comfort now as I imagine mom and dad are waltzing again all-around heaven, just as they did in our kitchen.

And then my little sister and I had one of those horrible sister arguments and did not talk for weeks. And then, one day, we had an impromptu phone conversation, and peace was made. The next week she had a headache she could not shake. Mom rushed her to the hospital. A double brain aneurysm ended her life, yet four others lived because of her gifted organs. God was merciful. I cannot imagine not heeding His heads up on forgiveness when the opportunity was presented. But I still do not think that guy was good enough for her…

She was only 46 and she had three beautiful children that are treasures in my heart. Two days later, I awoke to see all my dad flanked by my sisters standing together at the foot of my bed. I sat up, looked at them, and brokenheartedly I cried at them, "You left me! You did not even say goodbye!" They nodded as they understood the pain I was still reeling in and vanished. As my heart leaked out through my eyes, God was merciful and began my healing for them. I knew they were together and just fine. I know they loved Jesus. I know they not only made it to heaven but that they were escorted by God's angels. Scripture tells us that when we die, we will not be alone. Angels do accompany us on our journey when heaven calls us. In one of Jesus' parables, He talked about a poor man who suffered during his time on earth. When He died, Jesus said, "the angels carried him to Abraham's side" per Luke 16:22.

I still had my mom, Gloria Jeane, who had an incredibly traumatic life. Multiple car accidents, caused by others, broke her body many times, giving arthritis a way to invade the broken bits. Her neck. Her back. Her life. So much pain and she never complained but sang to

God, "Thank you, Jesus, today, is the day the Lord hath made, and I will rejoice in it and be glad." She watched her mate endure multiple heart attacks for too many years. She held her oldest daughter at her birth and at her death. She held her youngest daughter at her birth and at her death as well. She watched her son die slowly from the chemical abuses of Agent Orange. And through it all, she held her crippling arthritic pain up only to God while she ministered to others.

And me. She was my teacher. Many was the time I knew she was praying for me. I counted on it. And many was the time a letter was in the mailbox from her and in it was often a Word of Knowledge from God to me. They always started out "My blessed daughter," and would continue to how He saw me. He saw my distress. He saw my anguish. And made it aware that He was with me. Only the Holy Spirit could have shared particular knowledge of me with her for I too learned to hold my troubles to only God. In His mercy, God wanted to confirm that He knew. And if He knew, she knew. Take the time to call her and pray about it.

Love is shared.

Mom fought the wheelchair for 20 years. She had a deep and abiding faith like few I have ever seen. She literally fed many people, and in food, time and prayer. She saw miracles. She had a great laugh. She enjoyed her life, and she thanked Jesus for it all. She knew the secret to abundant life. She was a Kathryn Kuhlman and Corrie Ten

Boom student. My mother was so weak in her humanity that God filled her entirely, and together they made a difference in so many lives to meet Jesus.

I was privileged to be taught by her. She mentored me through many tragedies. She taught me to speak, "Thank you, Jesus, I praise you for this," even though. Together we saw miracles manifest from these words. Many laid claim to her time and attention, but she was my mom, and she loved me.

Her hospice care was short. The call at work came. I do not recall driving the distance, yet I remember hearing the song lyrics "nobody said it would be easy" on the radio. The devil is well, the devil. And he jogged my memory in this sad time of "remember when?" The memory of an act of jealousy, of my mother's time, by another's viciousness struck hard in a lie as a "concerned" person told my sister and I that we should not have been born, for our births threatened our mother's life. The carelessness in that statement haunted us for a long time and came blaring back. I gave the memory to Jesus. And He stepped in and saw that the truth was revealed as God granted me great mercy and removed all walls and boundaries and blessed me with the true vision of my birth.

I saw my mom reach for me. I saw myself looking into her eyes and felt unconditional love. I saw that she wanted me. I saw that she loved me, and she was glad I was born. This heavenly vision healed more than words could ever say in a single glimpse. My lifelong doubts left and peace filled my heart. It was her time to join the others that have already gone ahead and will soon be actively praising Jesus in total joy, without pain.

I crawled into the bed with her as I had always done, but there was no talking this time, just two souls bound by love and DNA. I told her it was okay to go; God would take care of me as He always did and not linger on my account. And boy, oh boy, did I know my mom! Even in her unconscious state, I knew she was waiting. And as her daughter, I knew exactly what for! She was waiting to be "officially" blessed to go. The nurses came into the room and prayed the Lord's Prayer over her. They blessed her life and ours. And she was gone. Her life's work is summed up in one act, "Nobody leaves without getting a blessing."

I left her room, walked outside, and leaned up against the pillar of red brick, made warm by the afternoon sun, of the Samaritan Home. It was late October on the prairie, and I knew that even this warmth was too fleeting. I sobbed as I wept for myself. I often wonder what God thought when he put the two of us together. Even though our dispositions are entirely alien to each other, we have the same eyes. And each time I look into the mirror, I see her eyes looking back at me. I recall the vision often, and I remember that she wanted me. This knowing has sustained me through living the rest of my life without her causing me to be the last one.

It was a beautiful October day, the kind that makes the calendars, and to the left of me was a field being harvested. The tractor purred along, collecting the seeds that had done their job of growing and maturing and were ready to be what their design intended. Letting the heat of the bricks warm my back, I felt my entire life flash in front of my eyes as I realized I was an orphan. And then, appearing in the almost vacant parking lot, an older gentleman was walking straight toward me. White hair. Bronzed face and hands. And sky-blue eyes. He asked, "Are you alright?" My voice caught in my throat, and the tears rolled down my cheeks like a thunderstorm. He reached out and hugged me tight and said, "you are loved, and you will be okay." Like in Luke 22:43, "An angel from heaven appeared to him and strengthened him."

And then he was gone. In that hug was an impartation from God as He took me back to my start and forged me forward to live out my legacy inherited from my mom, who was born to save the world, born to share the love of Jesus with everyone. Her prayers reached the ears of God and made a difference. She was an extraordinary woman living an extraordinary life, always on the go to meet the needs of others as a seer and a prophet. She knew of my day by looking at my face. I saw her take her final breath. In six be seeing my youngest granddaughter take her first. The legacy will continue. Less than a year after her mom passed, she joined her at the age of 82. God knows the plans He has for us. My daughter will tell her own story as she nurtures and mentors her daughters in our line, who will reap the legacy of generational blessings to continue to the glory of God.

Trade Secrets of a Seer

My children will preach to many of the mercies of Jesus. Their families will stand together with Jesus. I have asked the Father to fulfill this prophecy. It shall be done. In Jesus name, Amen.

Interesting note…on occasion, I have had visions of being in heaven before my birth, conversing with God, and assuring Him I would be okay as we contemplated my jumping into this life. He wasn't wrong; it has been fruitful. I would do it again and choose all the same people again. To them, I say, "Glory to God in the highest heaven, and on earth peace to those whom His favor rests." Luke 2:14. And then not long after my mom passed, my big brother succumbed to the lengthy destruction of the Viet Nam War's manifestation of Agent Orange, he did not deserve it. None of them did.

But just like in Job, God restores. Even though I lost, I found. Beauty out the ashes happen with God all the time. And joy replaces sorrow. It was a beautiful afternoon, and we were enjoying a nice lunch outside along the river. We ordered our meal, and as we waited, the granddaughters went to the river's edge to check things out. While playing, their sodas arrived, and I snuck the maraschino cherry out of one of the drinks. We hailed them both back, and they immediately noticed one was not like the other and asked me point blank, "Nana, did you take the cherry?" Without looking at them, I smiled and said, "nope!"

This "little" lie that I equivocated it to the same as teaching them how to blow the paper off the straw at each other was no more than out of my mouth when the napkin holder in front of me EXPLODED napkins. At me!! One after another after another!! Yes, the angels surely did let me know that not only did they hear, but God could also hear! Not okay!

But still… hahahahahaha, you got me, God. Ha! Like savoir faire, angels are everywhere! Sorry 'bout that, Lord.

And yet there was no condemnation in this experience, but the Father did use it to show me that joy was replacing sorrow. It was good to laugh. It opens the door to healing.

I am well aware of my shortcomings. And yes, it hurts my ego when the light goes on, illuminating all of them. Where the devil takes pleasure in my realizations that I am still quite a mess no matter how hard I try to stick to the path. It boggles my mind that Jesus only looks upon me with pure love and sees only His remarkable, unmarked child. The Song of Solomon sings, "You are altogether beautiful, my darling. There is no flaw in you." Even when I fall not just short of the glory of God but fall out of it altogether, it is to my chagrin to share this next story but share it I will.

I have become aware that one is never too old to channel their inner brat. With new job stress, weather delays, commuter problems after a day of computer problems, and winter here on the plains, I found myself on the verge of a tantrum at the gas pumps at the end of a very long day. Of all six pumps available, only two worked, and the snowmobilers were using those. What incurred next was truly divine intervention. I had an odd moment watching the others in the area watching me as I sat in my very nice, warm car, mouthing words with the mouth I kiss my grandchildren with. It had been a long day. I still had errands to do. It was getting dark out. It was so cold. The gas prices were crazy high and, and, and. And then when it was my turn, FINALLY! Adding insult to presumed injury, my pants got sprayed in a gasoline shower by a rogue gas hose. Argh! I topped off the tank, collected my receipt, ran into the market for milk, and fell flat on my face over the wrinkled rug. Oh, I am fine. Bruised knees, bruised ego... but lesson learned. "Message received, Lord. I will chill." My attitude was reinforced that I would get there when I got there and should just enjoy the show of here and now. I said a quick "thank you, Jesus," for realigning me with enough lessons in my life that I strive to learn more quickly. I wondered why God might have used this as a learning point and contemplated what was going on behind the spiritual scenes. Did He save me from a crash up the road? Did He save someone else by delaying me? Maybe. God only knows. He has His plans.

The facts are that God did not set me on the path to get sprayed by gasoline or allow me to trip over the rug. He is a good God. Fiercely gentle with His children. The Holy Spirit would never push me down either, as His desire is to lift us up. It was all just... me manifesting a lousy attitude into my own version of "karma."

Karma is a term based upon the principle of cause and effect and manifesting "what goes around comes around' and is snatched from the basic premise of the supernatural phenomena created by God, as stated in Galatians 6:7, "Be not deceived; God is not mocked: for whatsoever a man soweth, that shall he also reap. As well as in Job 4:8, "Even as I have seen, they that plow iniquity, and sow wickedness, reap the same."

Asked once, "How do you prove karma exists and if it has any effect on the wrongdoer's life if I see zero proof of it?" I simply answered, "Oh, just you wait!" So mind the words of you speak and the actions you take knowing as it says in Galatians 6:9, "And let us not grow weary of doing good, for in due season we will reap if we do not give up." It is just a matter of time for divine intervention to return to you what you give.

Remember! Good begets good like a boomerang.

## Secret Number 8 – Choose Whom You Serve

God is not kidding or patient on this. He is a jealous God and no way - no how - is He going to play second chair to anyone. He loves us. He deserves the same in return. I once mentored a lovely lady who needed a little help getting back on track to her path with Jesus. After weeks of talking and praying together in seeking God's help, I was given a vision of her kneeling in the center of a tower of books, and she was utterly engrossed in them. They were good books. All Christian-oriented, and she read to glean their knowledge to bolster her intellect to serve God better. She was eagerly looking forward to fulfilling a vision shared earlier with her of being a founding member of a sanctuary city for God's people on the run and could quickly populate its library with these books to help others. But at the end of the day, she was still dismayed as she could still not hear the voice of Jesus. She often fasted for days consuming only the words of these books.

I truly admired how hard she worked at it. She took Ecclesiastes 7:12 to heart, "For wisdom is a defense as money is a defense, but the excellence of knowledge is that wisdom gives life to those who have it." But she overlooked the wisdom in that reading the Bible helps us to discover our next step. "Your word is a lamp for my feet, a light on my path" from Psalm 119:105.

I was given a vision of this woman kneeling on her living room floor, encircled by a stack of books that almost touched the ceiling, beseeching God to hear His voice. And outside of this circle of books was her chair and a side table next to it. On the side table, I saw a book covered in dust. I suggest that we pray about it.

During the prayer, I was led to ask," If you had to choose, would you select the circle of books or the one on the table?" She asked, "Which one?" I said, "The one on the table beside your chair. It is covered in dust, and it appears to have a black cover." She then asked,

"You mean the Bible?" I replied, "It appears so." She said, "No, I cannot choose, I need all of them"

I felt sad for her as this uncompromising attitude may teach her that stubbornness is not a fruit of the Holy Spirit and subsequently realize God will not come in second or third place. But I know her to be a smart cookie, and I will continue to trust in God that she figures it out. The Holy Spirit never gives up on convicting us to do better. If not,

He will find someone who will comply. Of all the things we can compromise on our path, God, is not one of them. He made the very first commandment of the Ten Commandments as stated in Exodus 20, is love Him more than anything. The more you live this, the clearer you can hear Him and the more He will impart onto you. God has made it abundantly clear over my life span that not only does He always win, but He takes care of His own.

There's a bible story of Shadrach, Meshach, and Abednego that has been speaking loudly to me as the current media has once again declared itself king of the world, wanting us to kneel to the kingdom they are building. The bible story is about King Nebuchadnezzar, who built a monument that he decided was the new god. It was given to the current leading panel of experts and officials to carry out the decree that all shall worship it, determining who rule-followers were or rule breakers, and implement any consequences. Many being fearful of the repercussions of non-compliance and/or comfortable with their lot in life quickly got down on bended knees to the man-made idol because someone told them to. When compliance was seen, they called astrologers forward to denounce the Jews, and discrimination went into full swing against those who balked at the decree.

Just like then, there is a universal flaw that repeats itself in every generation where a handful of mere human beings build a kingdom and then strive at all costs to live forever as self-proclaimed deities, just as this King Nebuchadnezzar had. To secure their immortality, they command, coerce, bribe, or terrorize others to kneel and declare, "May the king live forever!"

And, in every generation, some will see that the emperor is wearing no clothes and refuse to abide by these mortal decrees and are subsequently "told on" by their peers. The non-conformists of King Nebuchadnezzar's time were rounded up and sentenced to death by fire unless they agreed to kneel to the thing. Three refused. They stood adamant in their faith in God, the only God, the Creator of the heavens and the universe. This same scenario has repeated itself throughout the reigns of Hitler, Mao Tse Tung, Napoleon, Saddam Hussein, Kim Jong Un I and II, Stalin, Emperor Hirohito, and others.

## Trade Secrets of a Seer

All familiar names.

The same neediness to be a god. The same immortality-driven agendas. But! God being God and our Protector, sent an angel into the furnace with the prisoners. The same God who stood with His people then, still does. He honored their words as spoken in Daniel 3:16 "...we do not need to defend ourselves before you in this matter, 17 If we are thrown into the blazing furnace, the God we serve can deliver us from it, and He will deliver us from Your Majesty's hand. 18 But even if He does not, we want you to know, Your Majesty, that we will not serve your gods or worship the image of your god..." This infuriated the king, and he set instructions to build a fire so hot that it burned the appointed prison guards. And yet Shadrach, Meschach, and Abednego did not sit in the fire scared, mopey and weepy but were seen unbound, unharmed, and walking around!

Three men went in. Four were seen. Three came out. And the King was convinced that, yes, absolutely their God existed. Part of me wonders if they were playing Bridge...

History repeats itself, yes, and the media populates the headlines with evil over good. And still, in the face of propaganda, these worst of the worst people and the others like them all failed in the end. They are ALL DEAD. They failed at not dying. The immortality they achieved is in disgust at their names and stories of the heroism of those who stood up to them and counted themselves children of God to defeat them. As I was doing my research, I read the story of one war survivor, Jan Ruff O' Hearne echoing the same thought, "By raping me, the Japanese took away everything from me - my self-respect, my dignity, my possessions, my family. I wonder how I coped. It's amazing how strong you can be. My strong belief in God and my faith and prayer helped me through."

Victimized people are often regular people, living ordinary lives, working to pay their bills, and feed their children. The stories that jump out at me are the ones of those who got through the hell-fires because they knew God. They knew His word, and they relied on their faith that He would help them weather the abuses heaped upon them or just maybe He would bring them home with Him. Either way, they had hope.

God is merciful with infinite patience, but we need to realize that He does not play the second chair. Like most people, weekends often become the focal point for sleeping in, attacking the to-do list hoping to fit in a little deserved fun, and the God stuff tends to get left at the bottom of the list. The Holy Spirit recently made me aware of my slacking, and all I could say was, "You caught me, God!

Yes, you sure did! I am so sorry, but I have an explanation. The last few days, I got busy. There were new projects, and that spring cleaning, and the yard work yada yada yada…"

How did He catch me up? I had a vision about a toothbrush. The more I used it, the more it felt odd in my mouth. I took it out and looked at it. It was a cheap knock-off, where you can get five in a package for less than a dollar a piece, and it was the wrong color! When I asked Him about this wrong toothbrush, my beloved Father, showed me the truth! It was not the one He gave me. I had been too busy to read the actual Bible and relied on getting by with smart apps and others' opinions. And oddly enough, right after this, two different people from opposite sides of the world sent me an out-of the-blue text that I was to read the Bible in its entirety ASAP. And to not just get through it looking for the blessings, but to read it so that God can get through to me as to what He has planned for me. With that twice shared instruction, I agreed.

And so, I had a conversation with the Holy Spirit about starting out this new quest with a new bible. And as I saw myself delving into it for the rest of my life, I asked for a turquoise leather one. Turquoise for pretty and leather for sturdy. And He said yes. I drove that day to the store to find it. And lo and behold, the book seller had rows upon rows of bibles! And the search began. And there it rested, the second shelf from the top, gleaming the warmest turquoise and I reached for it. Excitement faded as I saw the price.

$40! whoa! That's a lot! He said, "Buy it." I replied, "$40 is not in the budget for two more days." Again, He said, "Buy it." And so I did. They rang it up. I paid. I drove home. I stopped at the mailbox to get the day's mail and lo and behold! there was a check from a long-forgotten class action lawsuit for... yes! $40!

I opened my new bible and the page He pointed to, "Let the word of Christ dwell in you richly in all wisdom; teaching and admonishing one another in psalms and hymns and spiritual songs, singing with grace in your hearts to the Lord" from Colossians 3:16. He appreciates that I read the verse of the day and the meditation thoughts of another. But that is just it; they are not the Bible even though most of what I was reading was authored under His leadings.

And yes, the irony of this book is not lost on me, lol, but He asks me to read His word, absorbing His thoughts as it is my task to share His incredible love and point us all in the direction of Jesus. "For whatsoever things were written aforetime were written for our learning, that we through patience and comfort of the scriptures might have hope." Romans 15:4.

No, I did not feel any condemnation for putting the Bible time to the side. I did, however, feel that He missed me! And I missed Him! I changed my routine. I still read my Bible verse of the day before I get out of bed. And enjoy my daily meditations with my morning tea to get my mind right, getting the "gotta do's" out of my thoughts so I can take my time and spend my time reading the Bible. Out loud and to Him. He sits in the chair right across from me, and we talk. John 5:14 says, "This is the confidence we have in approaching God: that if we ask anything according to his will, he hears us." It is true just as it is written in Psalm 66, "I cried out to him with my mouth; his praise was on my tongue. If I had cherished sin in my heart, the Lord would not have listened; but God has surely listened and has heard my prayer.

> Praise be to God, who has not rejected my prayer or withheld his love from me!"

Even though it seemed I walked alone at times, I knew I did not. I learned that these trials had been my booster step up onto His lap and into His mercy. And now that I know this, I can point others to the shortcuts and straight on to Jesus, bypassing the worst of the scenic routes where comfort stations are limited. Because it is at God's convenience that I live to serve, I will trust in the Lord always as "He is my strength and my shield; in Him my heart trusts, and I am helped; my heart exults, and with my song, I give thanks to Him." Psalm 28:7.

And why is it such a big deal to read the Bible? So that you will stay okay.

So SUIT UP! Read your Bible! Out loud!

The Bible is designed to be heard. Time is short, and it appears the End of Days are upon us. Suit up? It is a hockey metaphor that means we are in a supernatural power play, and it is time to put into practice the training we have received and assist others in finding Jesus.

## Secret Number 9 - Forgiveness Heals

I have been asking God about an ongoing observation that pops up like a stem of poison ivy in bloom amongst cultivated roses. And just what is it? What the heck is with the scowling, muttering, bitter people whose countenance gives visualization to the word crone?! If you search the 'net to define crone, you find... "Since the late fourteenth century, the word has been an impolite term describing an old and bad-tempered woman or man. In fairytales, one is called a crone as a once beautiful human female turned ugly in spirit by a tragedy through witchcraft."

The Bible says in 2 Corinthians 9:7, "Each of you should give what you have decided in your heart to give, not reluctantly or under compulsion, for God loves a cheerful giver."

Just what is the lesson in crone versus a cheerful giver?

When we walk with Jesus, others will know Him by our love. They will see His countenance upon our faces. In our words. In our deeds. We are His billboard of truth.

We know this, yet there are still those who wish to say, "I am fed up with people, with trying, with family, with friends, with the whole thing!" Hey! That is more than okay! Jesus still died on the cross for them and us. He cares if we feel lonely or have been betrayed, or just do not feel good. He cares that we have chosen not to choose anymore.

He watches as we have sentenced ourselves to a self-imposed prison. He has others who fill in the voids we create. He loves enough. In Him, there is hope, peace, and joy! Even if.

Not feeling it? Move closer to Him. Skooch on over just a bit. He is more than happy, willing, and able to take up whatever is burdening our hearts, whatever is chaining our thoughts to a cold cell, whatever has hurt us enough that it has crippled desires. He can give us back the rest of our lives to live abundantly! Give it a go. We are still breathing and on this side of the grave. Try! One more time. Let your sweet self back out to play. We need our good selves. Jesus needs us. There are ways to minister to others that only we can do.

Yes, you too! Just say, "Fix me, Father." He will. Ask the Holy Spirit to help you. In Mark 1:8, John the Baptist baptized the people in the Jordan River, saying, "I baptize you with water, but He, Jesus, will baptize you with the Holy Spirit." This, too, is at our invitation, and He has helped me understand that I, like you, have a designed purpose in being here. "Are not two sparrows sold for a penny? Yet not one of them will fall to the ground apart from the will of your Father. So do not be afraid; you are worth more than many sparrows." Matthew 10:29-31 and to Jesus... we matter. It is a given.

We are not in this place, at this time, by accident or a fluke, and we are where we are to be, for now. The Holy Spirit comes with a fire to quench our carnal nature into a spiritual one that changes our outcome and propels us forward to good and right things while the calls from the dark side lose their wooing strengths. Rest assured that while we are here, the Holy Spirit is the Comforter, the Teacher, the One True Helper who will always point our way to Jesus, showing us why we were born and our mission of love.

Should we choose to accept it, our mission is to help others realize that we all have a reason to be here, and we all are a part of God's kingdom, and it is a tremendous honor to help others on their paths to heaven.

John 13:34, "A new command I give you: Love one another. As I have loved you, so you must love one another." As for the feeling… for me… when I pray in tongues, sing along to worship music, paint, or blog my lessons, I get a catch in my throat, tears well up in my eyes, and the knowledge of just how grateful I am that Jesus loves me envelops all of me with hope, while at other times, I can sit quietly and just be. I learned this is my ministry, hope in, hope out. We each matter. We each make a difference.

Even in their incarceration, the disciples, Paul and Silas, prayed and sang hymns in the company of the other prisoners. They waited on God and enjoyed their timeout. And then! God rocked a violent earthquake at midnight, shaking the foundations of the prison, which caused the prison doors to fly open and all prisoner's chains to break, but they stayed with their jailer. In gratitude, the jailer took them home, fed them, washed their wounds, and he and all his household were baptized by Paul and Silas. The magistrates sent their officers to the jailer with the order: "Release those men." With that, they were allowed to leave and to go in peace.

Trade Secrets of a Seer

In forgiving others… so just what exactly is required?

He said, "Be like Me." He did not say, "Right now and be perfect at it," but He wants us to strive for it. When the threat of offenses rears its ugly head, we are to look at it and ask Jesus how to see this mountain for what it is and keep our eyes still on His face even though He knows that this is one of the hardest jobs in a Christian's job description.

It is a big deal to forgive others who trespass all over our lives.

Jesus repeatedly taught that if we want to be forgiven by God, then we must forgive others in Matthew 6. He shared the parable of the unforgiving servant in Matthew 18 who lost his pardon because he did not forgive others, emphasizing the law that not to forgive another is an unforgivable sin. It would be easier to wear the "Get-Along" shirt some give to their fighting children, but we are not children anymore. We are warriors in training for the upcoming tribulation.

And now for the hard part… forgiving ourselves. I once came across a family in the next lane in a mini-van at a gas station. As the father got out to fuel up, his little girl leaped out after him just as he shut the door. Yes. Her fingers were caught in it. She screamed. He ran to open the door; we ran to our cooler in the back and brought him the bag of ice we had just purchased. She was sobbing. He was distraught. Mom was just coming out of the station, I looked at him and said, "your little girl will be okay, she was lucky and will soon forget the pain, but unfortunately, you will not. Like most parents, you will remember this for the rest of your life. Just remember as well that it was just an accident. Be easy on yourself."

It was just an accident. It could have happened to anyone. Whether we get hurt by our own traumas or dramas or by someone else, we can be healed by Jesus just as soon as we ask as a child of God. But the key to this healing is the acceptance of it. And the accepting part is often achieved by self-purpose. What is in it for us to be healed and let the pain go?

It is not in our best interest to hold on to it as it creates a wall between ourselves and God. And where there are walls, grace is hard to find. Blessings? Even harder. And if we cannot hear God, how are we supposed to interpret the signs and wonders accurately He gives us without them being tainted by our imagination or ego? We will be like those who say, "At 11:11 pm on this day, if you do this, and then you tithe this to this person, I am pretty sure that God is going to pay off your entire mortgage because I saw 1-2-3-4 four times in three hours two weeks ago." Ummm... no, not of God at all. Now that being said... there are ways that God does communicate via the numerical, be it 444, 1111, etc. as in His mercy He will make Himself known to you. Double check the source, be kind to yourself and finish your walk giving credibility to your faith in Jesus that your life and way of thinking have changed.

And this leads to the other part of the "why not forgive yourself?" Heed the Proverbs, the original motivational book on gaining wisdom, and see how not to be foolish or its derivatives are mentioned over 100 times. Ha! Those who travel their lives holding on to guilt are easily deceived, and the wicked will prey upon it. it and looking to line their pockets with the proceeds.

Of course, the memory will try to reinvade our peace. But that does not mean we have to accept it or see it as permission to wallow in it. Choose instead to focus on that self-forgiveness meets a definite and divine purpose.

Mercifully for us, the crucifixion of Jesus happened, and all of mankind came under the grace of God. Paul encourages in Ephesians 4:32 all believers in Christ Jesus to "Be kind to one another, tenderhearted, forgiving each other, just as God in Christ also has forgiven you". In Colossians 3:12-13, he writes, "So as those who have been chosen of God, holy and beloved, put on a heart of compassion, kindness, humility, gentleness, and patience; bearing with one another, and forgiving each other, whoever has a complaint against anyone; just as the Lord has forgiven you, so also should you forgive others.

Encouraging? And God is not demanding it? So why forgive any at all then?

Why is it more satisfying to hang on to those hurts and slights than to let them go?

Because it is our human nature to drift away from God and create idols to cling to, with offenses being at the top of the pile.

- You can only have one master. Jesus. Or what was.
- You can look at Jesus. Or what was.
- You can choose to walk with chains, or you can choose to leave them behind to what was.

Jesus will love you either way, but it depends on how you spend your days and what your epitaph will read. It can either say, "I did it my way and look at where I am," or "I spent my life following Jesus and it is Paradise for me now." Try. Be forgiving. Jesus wants this freedom for you. That should be enough.

A post has been making the rounds on social media asking for forgiveness for all transgressions to whoever happens across it. I read it and looked at the person posting and thought, "nope, we are good! no problems here," happily and moved on. But the thoughts moved on with me. And then the questions with Jesus started.

- Can I forgive a person who doesn't know that they have wronged me?
- If they do not ask for forgiveness, can forgiveness proceed?
- What if I die before I forgive them, or they ask?

## Trade Secrets of a Seer

Anyone who would hurt you is your enemy at that moment, and whether it is either in ignorance or intentional is a moot point. Luke 6:27 clearly states, "But I say to you who hear, Love your enemies, do good to those who hate you, 28 bless those who curse you, pray for those who abuse you." Why is it so hard and unfathomable to ask another, "Will you forgive me? I was in a lunatic moment, and I know I hurt you? I am so sorry."

We ask forgiveness from Jesus all the time.

Why do we not ask another?

We have all been hurt so many times by family, friends, and strangers. And yet, because God is good, He uses these situations as lessons in giving mercy and grace as we move up the path together. We are to leave unpleasant situations like the man Lot did in not looking back, or at the slight and to certainly not embrace it as his wife did, but rather adhere to Matthew 10:14, "And whosoever shall not receive you, nor hear your words, when ye depart out of that house or city, shake off the dust of your feet." Do not worry about them. You worry about yourself. He's got them. Let Him have you. So if forgiveness, either giving or asking, never happens, understand your role in His church.

"Can't we just all get along?" would be great but is not realistic. We do not have to be friends, but we are to be loving. Best case scenario? Just be polite and do not let hate mess up your day. Count on the love that conquers all, Jesus. Ask Him to help you see "them" as He sees "them." Hate left unchecked in our attention makes hate far more critical, which sets in the decay of our hearts. It destroys the foundation like ants tunneling under it. Imagine, if you will, a magician with his hat ready to produce an illusion with a trick of the eye or sleight of hand. Depending on where you sit affects your perspective of what is true.

There was an instance when I got hit with a two-fer at a gathering! Two different people, both obnoxious and obvious about their disdain for me. I am unaware of their reasoning, and I could have called attention to it. I could have said something, but in the end, what would it matter? No one wins as hate causes pain that is not easily forgotten or forgiven. And as time goes by, the negative feeling takes over the murkiness of the experience, which has deliberately set out to distort the truth. What I did do was tell Jesus about them. I told Him what they said, what they did, and how they made me feel. And I laid them at the cross. I made them His problem. All I asked in return was for me to see them as He sees them, which takes some effort on my part.

That basket for troubles I put at the base of the cross eons ago is actually more the size of a grocery cart, but it carries me through the days when I treat offenses like a perverted hobby, with well-greased wheels as it is way too easy to roll it back when I decide that maybe I should push it for a while. I wonder if God ever rolls His eyes… lol.

I found out later that one was in excruciating pain over a betrayal caused to her, and the other actually hates everybody. I was not singled out or receiving "special treatment". I am grateful that God helped me keep my mouth shut. It was a good day to be done with it all, and it did not propel me into yet another lesson.

Or so I thought. Ha! I had dreamed the alarm system went off in our home. I saw myself attempting to switch on the lights but could not. The dream unfolded to where I saw my husband enter the basement to yell, "what are you doing here? How did you get in?" And there stood these same two people covered in ants. Ewww! Ants, the symbol of my annoyances, I actually burdened them with. Oh, not good! I awoke and prayed in the Spirit to praise Jesus and ask for forgiveness. I felt a vortex of Godly love radiating the entire room. Yay! And then God showed me Luke 6:

- If you love those who love you, what credit is that to you? Even sinners love those who love them.
- If you do good to those who do good to you, what credit is that to you? Even sinners do the same.
- If you lend to those from whom you hope to receive back, what credit is that to you? Even sinners do the same.

So instead, we are to love our enemies, do good, and lend, hoping for nothing in return; and our reward will be great, and you will be sons of the Most High. For He is kind to the unthankful and evil. Yes, we are to be merciful, just as our Father is merciful.

To which I once said to my precious Lord and Savior, "Them? Noooo! Anybody else, Please!"

He says, "Yes, them."

Even people who have served the Lord for years still trip up on this one. I had the moment of clarity to question, "What is there worth hating so much that it will keep me from heaven?"

Nothing! We are allowed to only enter paradise through God's grace via His son, Jesus Christ, who lived and died for us once we accepted Him into our hearts and our lives. Continuing the hate will not only add to and lengthen our lessons here but will repel all joy away from us. God is love.

In Him, there is no condemnation for anything or anyone. Not even for worshipping our own pain. To a point... And then there is the "happiness" scale that we would all like to ping at a nine or ten all the time where our peace is destroyed because "they hurt my feelings" or "somebody said something." This is a superficial peace that relies on our pride and our ego. To be restored back into the true peace of God, we need to recognize this pride factor and ask for His forgiveness.

And then..., knowing that this all too ingrained human issue is neither lethal nor contagious, practice staying away from things that reflect back to ourselves and instead look outward.

- Notice stuff. People, places, things, times, events.
- Find God's people.
- Watch and observe the scenarios that play out in others.
- Take a second look at those people who stand behind the counters or on the street corners holding their signs. Stop and notice kids playing.
- Listen to the sounds around you.
- Shut your eyes when you eat ice cream.
- Bury your face in a whole bouquet of flowers and inhale.
- Do a crossword puzzle and give your brain a break.
- And so on…

All these things feed your soul while removing ego out of focus. Why? How? Because we live in a wonderful world with lots of wonderful people and it all hums right along and welcomes your observations as well as your participation. And sooner or later contentment aligns itself in your habits. The flip side of this coin, should you choose not to, is illness in some form.

You have heard of the idiom "worried sick" right? Well, did you know that offenses can also make you ill? Being created by God, we thrive in a positive atmosphere. Offenses are based upon pride, insecurities, etc. which all conflict with God's basics. And walls go up preventing us from hearing God and the devil loves it!

## Trade Secrets of a Seer

Many illnesses linger because of worshipped hurts. I recall a 1960s television sitcom regarding a neighbor who "enjoyed poor health for years." Something seemed to have had happened to her, and she never got over it. To protect herself, she became "ill". It was then how she interacted with others it became her stardom. It was her excuse and reason, and she lived comfortably if not a bit delighted in her misery. And I began to be aware of just how many really "choose" this way of "life" not because of any specific disease but out of emotional pain, loneliness, and much-needed attention.

To this day, I am still perplexed by this because Jesus really does heal!! And we do "get what you say." Just as good begets good, evil begets evil. This command for illness for attention is an abomination of the gift of life. Our troubles are lessons in overcoming and sending us out with empathy to help others. They are keys to finding out exactly why we were born, what makes us tick and what we can do for someone else. Had she forgiven the offender, she might have found a truer stardom rather than a substitute. When we settle for less, we hold heaven at bay which in turn holds our anointing's at bay.

Ecclesiastes… A time to be born. A time to die. I have been grieving for a long, long time. "Nobody knows the trouble I've seen. Nobody knows my sorrow," still sings the song. Nobody knows. And for a long time, grief was my most significant testimony. At times I wondered if it had become like a false god or my own claim to fame. I certainly did not want that to be my notecard for conversation-starting.

Trade Secrets of a Seer

My true testimony is that I survived many losses and trials via the grace of God. I lost my people, yes. It was and still is heart-wrenching. A simple celebration of "National Sibling Day" or "Sisters Day" on social media can bring me to my knees with "Lord, it is so not fair!" But my testimony that is all mine is this; I loved, and I lost. And Jesus walked with me through all of them. I know where my family is, and I am pleased for them. They knew Jesus! They are with Him now. And when it is my time, I will see them again. I did not blame God, I questioned Him on it, but the blame belongs to the evil in this world. Mom always said, "It's a wicked, wicked world. Thank God we have Jesus."

My testimony is that I learned that people that go throughout life as naturally faulty. To hope another can genuinely understand your plight will only send the both of you down the rabbit hole. Confusion can set in and brings along misunderstandings, accusations, blame, bitterness, etc. all vying to mess up our faith causing an open path for the wall of un-forgiveness to barricade in.

I have found that the only one who can is God. He understands. He even promised in Revelation 21:4, "He will wipe every tear from their eyes, and death shall be no more, neither shall there be mourning, nor crying, nor pain anymore, for the former things have passed away." He does. I can testify. I learned that I also needed to wipe away my own tears so I can see Him better. I learned that I needed to quit complaining about my lot so I could hear Him better. I learned that the grief process takes as long as it takes like when the grands ask, "When is Papa going to be home?" and I tell them, "Dark thirty." It also rolls in like waves over the simplest of causes. I came upon my dad's once-favorite candy in a store, and grief swept in, leaving me bereft, again. God saw this. Because He is incredibly merciful and a Father, He immediately evoked images into my thoughts of happier times and bonus-ed me with the comforting memory of dad's aftershave aroma to ride out the current storm long enough to check out and get to my car. Two things I strive for, no crying at work and no crying in the store.

After a time of grieving, there are those who grow tired of our sorrowed state of being, wondering how the hurt can linger and not understanding that there is no "walking it off." Be aware the shock of those being like the woe-be- gone Job's own miserable comforters can cause un- forgiveness to prick our heart.

God does not get tired of our grief and reminds us that even His son, Jesus, took eternal death from us. Of course, we will see them again, and yes, they are safe with Him in Heaven and are cheering you on, as in Matthew 22:32, "I am the God of Abraham, and the God of Isaac, and the God of Jacob? God is not the God of the dead, but of the living."

Yes, if they knew Jesus, rest assured they are indeed living the high life. "Blessed are those who mourn, for they shall be comforted" by the Holy Spirit, and straight out, as it says in Matthew 5:4. God never permits us to seek or speak to the dead via seances or mediums or the saints.

They cannot help. The Bible tells us, "Man is destined to die once and after that to face judgment." It is of no use to ask them to speak to us, just as it is pointless to pray for their soul. Their life here is done. We are to pray for the living.

My daughter was worrying on my chronic state of grief and asked if I would talk to a friend of hers, a rather old but very nice, retired man of God. I agreed, and we met. He said, "I hear you have had some losses. Tell me about them." And I started rattling off their names like a grocery list when he interrupted me to say that I was just listing names. Ha! Clever man! He saw right through that. He paused and then looked me in the eye and said, "Which one hurts the most?" I blurted out, "My dog!" And I was awash in guilt!

He said, "It's okay! You had already left your family to live your life, and your dog was part of that life." Even though losing each of these people became markers in my life, I am propelled each day to begin by reading my Bible aloud. I have learned to twirl away grief like a child in a pink sequined tutu in this practice. I have learned to duck rather than flinch. I am content, grateful, and happy. I love my life and those I allow in it.

And that there is the biggest secret right, to be particular in who I let in. God instructs us to love all people and to care for those in our circle. But we are not mandated by Him to like all of them, and we have the free choice of who we choose to be in our circle. Huge revelation for me! Yes, He will send others in to us with a message or send us out to others with the offer of love but staying is a choice.

We have the choice that every day can be a good day. Every morning speak out loud, "This is the day the Lord has made; I will rejoice and be glad in it' as it is essential to seek out the positive and to realize that all people have the potential to seek happiness because of Jesus.

Happiness…that seemingly elusive fibromyalgia of all the emotions that hide in plain sight every time we take our eyes off of Jesus and focus on our circumstances. To just trust Jesus, He will show you how true it is that all things are possible for those who love the Lord. And He desires to see us thrive and prosper in every way, overcome the "issues," and move on. The friction of holding on so tight to offenses or dragging one's feet in rebellion rather than letting go pushes us deeper into the rut. Now mind you, like habits, ruts can be comfortable but are of little use to Jesus.

They will fester and grow of their own accord unless we give them deliberately to God. Try not to let your pride go up as a wall preventing you from receiving all of God's blessings.

So yes, we think we forgave and forgot and moved on, but the telltale sign that we clung to a bit of the offense is that a similar situation will present itself, and the memory will emerge. The justification will ensue. The excuses happily resurface. Ahh, but now we are older. No more bottle baby faith, and we should be mature enough and knowledgeable enough to be more amenable to God's ways when we seek His help to overcome "the reasons," just as the Holy Spirit's convictions persist. Good on us! Oswald Chambers said,

"Conviction of sin is one of the rarest things that ever strikes a man. It is the threshold of an understanding of God. Jesus Christ said that when the Holy Spirit came, He would convict of sin. When the Holy Spirit rouses the conscience and brings him into the presence of God, it is not his relationship with men that bothers him, but his relationship with God." John 16:8, "When he [the Holy Spirit] comes, he will convict the world, and show where right and wrong and judgment lie. He will convict them of wrong…"

Look at it. Take a good look. Say goodbye and finally give the mess to God. He can handle it. There's a basket, or a grocery cart, at the base of His cross, just waiting for all your woes. You know the one. Isn't it time? It isn't too late for God to have a plan for us, and it is a good plan! We will surely like it better than our own. We just need to try and cooperate. It's got to be pretty good if it is coming from Him.

"For I know the plans I have for you," declares the Lord, "plans to prosper and not to harm you, plans to give you hope and a future." Jeremiah 29:11

Trade Secrets of a Seer

## Secret Number 10 – Don't Get Left Behind

The lesson is easy. Time is short. The story's message is short, and the story ends where nobody gets out of here alive. Where you go from here, heaven or hell depends on what you do now. I have lived long enough to have heard, "We are in a living hell right here and right now." True enough. Our beautiful, wonderful world is under the current reign of evil that battles for our immortal souls, and we are all in a spiritual dress rehearsal for our lives. The actual show starts where we choose our seats, be it in heaven by choice or hell by default.

I know that people claim to have had NDE, near-death experiences, and many were fortunate in that they received a second change to choose Jesus. One of my extended family members had this NDE caused during a heart attack. He returned from surgery, and according to him, from the gate of hell to describe what he experienced, that hell is real and that he beheld its horrors. He came out of this experience no longer taking for granted that he had time and could get straight with Jesus before his time here was truly up. He came out of the hospital and came over to have a long heart to heart talk with my dad. Before he left, they prayed the Sinner's Prayer together and he came to the understanding that it is only accepting in faith that Jesus' death and resurrection washed away our sins by the blood He shed for us for we are all sinners and we all fall short of the Glory of God.

## The Sinner's Prayer

"God, I know that I am a sinner. I know that I deserve the consequences of my sin. However, I am trusting in Jesus Christ as my Savior. I believe that His death and resurrection provided for my forgiveness. I trust in Jesus and Jesus alone as my personal Lord and Savior. Thank you, Lord, for saving me and forgiving me! Amen!"

The whole purpose of receiving any gift from God is to share the hope of Him. He wants everybody to spend eternity with Him. Jesus weeps now for those who have already turned away. But the time will come when it all ends and the gates to heaven close and hells gates open wide to those who heard the words from our Savior, "I never knew you."

Do not get left behind. Getting separated from our loves will always lurk. It is a bane to all of us. It shakes our faith by the fear it evokes. Genesis straight up says, "For you are dust, and to dust, you shall return." It should cause us to be that much more grateful. Jesus taught me that nothing is as valuable as "right now," "this time," "this discussion," and indeed, "no point of view" was ever worth leaving a conversation lacking love. I now stand not in grief, yet it lingers and flares, but all in honor of my family and knowing I will most certainly get out of here alive because I walk with Jesus.

## Trade Secrets of a Seer

I see those who are too busy to make the phone call. I see those who choose politics over family. I see those who choose drugs and alcohol over those that love them. I see those who taunt God. I see those who "guess" they will be going to heaven. I see those who think they comprehend Jesus. I see, and I say to myself, you just do not know what you do not know until it happens to you. Once we are dead, there are no more chances. And the dead do not speak. Demons do. But not the dead. They are sent to hell or to heaven It is also too late to pray for their souls, and things said and done cannot be taken back.

Tomorrow is a crapshoot. Do you feel lucky? I KNOW I will see my family again. Isaiah 9:2, "The people that walked in darkness have seen a great light: they that dwell in the land of the shadow of death, upon them hath the light shined." I have. And Jesus is my light.

On Judgement Day, we will each stand-alone before God to testify to the character we played in the life we were given. Liken it to sitting alone on an empty stage with a silent microphone. The spotlight is on you alone. The curtains are parted. The assignment is easy as you understood your part in Romans "14: 11, for it is written, "As I live, says the Lord, every knee shall bow to me, and every tongue shall confess to God." 12 So then each of us will give an account of himself to God."

It will happen. For it clearly states in 2 Corinthians 5:10, "For we must all appear before the judgment seat of Christ; that every one may receive the things done in his body, according to that he hath done, whether it be good or bad," and He will ask you one question, "Does my son, Jesus, know you?" This is no time for an "I hope so" or "I think so." But no worries, mate. Jesus will answer for you.

Matthew 7:21, "Not every one that saith unto me, Lord, Lord, shall enter into the kingdom of heaven; but he that doeth the will of my Father which is in heaven. 22 Many will say to me in that day, Lord, Lord, have we not prophesied in thy name? and in thy name have cast out devils? and in thy name done many wonderful works 23 And then will I profess unto them, I never knew you: depart from me, ye that work iniquity."

Or will you experience Luke 23:43, "And Jesus said to him, "Assuredly, I say to you, today you will be with Me in Paradise." And then maybe, just maybe, some of us will get out of here alive through the mercy of the Rapture where the righteous children of God will escape the coming apocalypse, or the Revelation of not the end, but the beginning of the end where the easiest part will be the world wars, the global disasters, pandemics will be where the chaff will be separated from the wheat to endure the worst of times when Satan reveals his true self to those who were deceived by the charismatic Antichrist.

But God is God. God always wins. And God not only takes care of His own, He raises them to life in His kingdom.

# Trade Secrets of a Seer

Soliloquy by Denise Rand Dahlheimer

## Trade Secrets of a Seer

I was working on my Holy Spirit-inspired oil-paint piece called Rapture, Shakespeare by Sunflowers, of a sunflower whose petals gave way to the winds inspired by

1 Peter 1:24, "because "All flesh is as grass and all the glory of man as the flower of the grass. The grass withers and its flower falls away, and this is the word preached unto you by the gospel."

The piece started out as a simple sunflower with petals intact, that soon gave way to the petals being cast to the wind as in 1 Peter 1:24, "For, All people are like grass, and all their glory is like the flowers of the field; the grass withers and the flowers fall."

Shylock reacted out of his deep pain, nee vengeance, wanting to outdo the evil that had been done to him and would sink to his abuser's level of inhumanity when he spoke, "I am a Jew. Hath not a Jew's eyes? Hath not a Jew hands, organs, dimensions, senses, affections, passions; fed with the same food, hurt with the same weapons, subject to the same diseases, healed by the same means, warmed and cooled by the same winter and summer as a Christian is? If you prick us, do we not bleed? If you tickle us, do we not laugh? If you poison us, do we not die? And if you wrong us, shall we not revenge? If we are like you in the rest, we will resemble you in that. If a Jew wrongs a Christian, what is his humility? Revenge. If a Christian wrongs a Jew, what should his sufferance be by Christian example? Why, revenge. The villainy you teach me I will execute, and it shall go hard, but I will better the instruction."

Shylock's desire to return evil for evil and pain for pain offers no satisfaction or healing except further damage to his soul. His thoughts paralleled ongoing trouble that reared its ugly head again in my life and tried to steal my peace. Somebody said something... as I contemplated it with Jesus, I noticed the sunflower's petals clinging tightly to the base of the flower as the offenses and the people tied to them. I gave them one by one back to God, reciting, "It no longer matters. It matters not. It no longer matters. It matters not..."

Rapture, Shakespeare by Sunflowers by Denise Rand Dahlheimer

## Trade Secrets of a Seer

In surrendering the injustices and seeking only to be one with God, my petals were not just cast into the wind but raptured out of the problem per His grace given in Romans 12:19 Dearly beloved, avenge not yourselves, but rather give place unto wrath: for it is written, Vengeance is mine; I will repay, saith the Lord. 20 Therefore if thine enemy hunger, feed him; if he thirsts, give him drink: for in so doing thou shalt heap coals of fire on his head. (as shown as the coals burning an abyss into the flower's head) 21 Be not overcome of evil but overcome evil with good.

Interestingly, the term "rapture" is not found in the Bible. According to W.W. Skeat's "Etymology of the English Language, 1879", "rapture" was coined by William Shakespeare, taking from Latin's "to be transported by a lofty emotion or ecstasy from the word "raptus." Which does align with 1 Thessalonians 4:17, "Then we which are alive and remain shall be caught up together with them in the clouds, to meet the Lord in the air: and so shall we ever be with the Lord."

In my own life, trouble was currently attempting to rear its ugly head when somebody said something offensive. As I contemplated it with Jesus, I noticed the paintings' flower petals, hanging tight to their seeded base, just as the offenses I was clinging to. I gave them back to God with "it no longer matters. It matters not. It no longer matters. It matters not..."

And I saw the lesson of the sunflower whose face always follows the sun.

Trade Secrets of a Seer

So with that, here's your sign.

Keep Going by Denise Rand Dahlheimer

Each feather is a blessing, a unique gift of God. Psalms 91:11, "For he will command his angels concerning you to guard you in all your ways…" show our heavenly Father giving His angels commands concerning the protection and guardianship of us, His beloved children. Angels always move to the authority and sound of God's voice.

In Jeremiah 29:11, For I know the plans I have for you," declares the LORD, "plans to prosper you and not to harm you, plans to give you hope and a future.

Until the other side then. Blessings to you and yours from Number 6:

24 The Lord bless thee, and keep thee:

25 The Lord make his face shine upon thee,

and be gracious unto thee:

26 The Lord lift up his countenance upon thee,

and give thee peace.

27 And they shall put my name upon the children of Israel,

and I will bless them.

In Jesus Name, Amen.

## Author Bio

For a long time, I found the slogan "nobody rides for free" of the 1970s relatable, almost my motto. The more in tune I become with Jesus, I see "letting go and letting God" from the 1960s worldwide Holy Spirit Charismatic Movement more "right on!" as it pushes me forward to finding Him in the meaning of my life. And do you know what I found? That I am a prophetic  manifestation of God's imagination, and Jesus has blessed me abundantly with healings, opportunities, and love.

This collection of stories is a taste of my lessons as I entreated mountains of evil, brutality, betrayal, divorce, remarriage, grieving, loss, success, sweetness, love, faith, and endurance in day-to-day living with others. Each day I start new. Not anew, for anew is starting over. But new as in "this day IS a brand-new day!

I am a child of God, baptized of water in Jesus and anointed in the fire of the Holy Spirit, making these the best choice I have ever made.

I know where I am going; I also know to whom I am going. I do not walk this life alone; I walk with Jesus, for I am a seer seeing visions and dreams via the Holy Spirit and blessed to see with His spiritual eyes.

I was born with the talents of an artist combined with the gift of seeing the supernatural sides of life. I paint and write about the prophetic visions I am shown by the Holy Spirit when I pray. Together, we exhale works of these visions and dreams from inhaling God's grace. I write their stories as symbols of hope as a road map back to Him. I am delighted to "Follow after charity, and desire spiritual gifts, but rather that ye may prophesy." 1 Corinthians 14:1.

I am a wife who chose well, the second time. Three decades and more later, he still makes my heart happy. Are we perfect? For each other, yes. I am a mom of two and grateful they were born. I am very proud of them as they grew up to be independent strivers rather than survivors. The effects of some of my choices caused their life to be a lot harder, initially, but God saw us through, and yet without those choices, I would not have them. I once told my daughter, "I am so sorry that I either over-watered you or under- watered you. The fact that I had water at all was by the grace of God." In her mercy, she replied, "You water me just enough so that I was able to find water on my own." And indeed, she did!

I am a grandmother of seven and all are treasures in my heart. Yes, I still would have chosen my children first.

Leaving the room on a high note… none of these secrets are really secrets. The more you walk with Jesus, the more you know.

Thank you for walking with me on my path. I am grateful that I can share how I got back to my start and moved forward. Be blessed and until the other side then. ~Denise Rand Dahlheimer

Trade Secrets of a Seer

Trade Secrets of a Seer

Book 2 Preview: Hope Uninterrupted

## Entreating God's Open Portal Policies

Messages of uninterrupted hope from heaven as I found my soul purpose to being here.

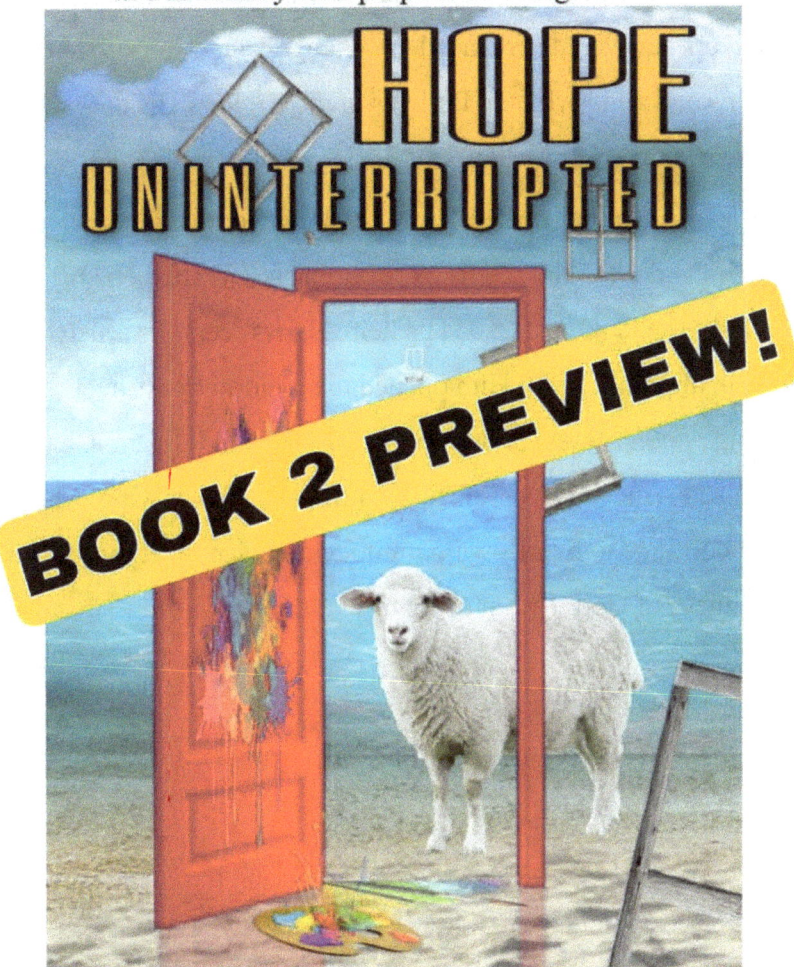

**BY DENISE RAND DAHLHEIMER**

A SUPERNATURAL ARTIST WHO FOUND THE OPEN DOOR

**About the Cover**

Jesus said in Mark 9:23, "If you can believe, all things are possible to them that believe."

Christianity is not a carrot-on-a-stick philosophy. The answers we seek from God are not out there somewhere hovering. God wants to take care of our here and now's. If we want to see the manifestation of prayers answered, we need to change our mindset, renew our thoughts and align with the Policies in the Bible as His doors, and the windows and find out what He will say yes to.

In Hope Uninterrupted, I share how God taught me to walk through the door and into His expectation as I applied His principles. I not only found myself to be His heiress, His seer, His artist, and that living in alignment with Him opened the windows of heaven, pouring blessings upon blessings onto me in vision's and dream's, answered prayer's, divine intervention, anointing's, and knowing why I am here. I continue to overflow in gratitude and want everyone to see the faithfulness of God. I want us all to win this round.

## Credits & Concordance

- Abrahamic Covenant: The Abrahamic Covenant is an unconditional covenant. The actual covenant is found in Genesis 12:1–3. The ceremony recorded in Genesis 15 indicates the unconditional nature of the covenant. When a covenant was dependent upon both parties keeping commitments, then both parties would pass between the pieces of animals. In Genesis 15, God alone moves between the halves of the animals. Abraham was in a deep sleep. God's solitary action indicates that the covenant is principally His promise. He binds Himself to the covenant. Source: https://www.gotquestions.org/Abrahamic-covenant.html

- Baader-Meinhof phenomenon: (aka the Red Car Syndrome) is a Frequency illusion, also known as the Baader–Meinhof phenomenon or frequency bias, is a cognitive bias in which, after noticing something for the first time, there is a tendency to notice it more often, leading someone to believe that it has a high frequency of occurrence. It occurs when increased awareness of something creates the illusion that it is appearing more often. Source: https://en.wikipedia.org/wiki/ Frequency_illusion

- Bible references: King James Version (KJV), New King James Version (NKJV) and New International Version are used for scripture.

- Billy Graham: William Franklin Graham Jr. (1918 – 2018) was an American evangelist and an ordained Southern Baptist minister. Source: https://billygraham.org

- Bob Jones: Robert Reynolds Jones Sr. (1883 - 1968) an American evangelist, pioneer religious broadcaster, and the founder and first president of Bob Jones University. Source: http://www.bobjones.org

- Carte Blanche: Full discretionary power. Merriam-Webster Dictionary

- Cause and effect: The relationship between two things when one thing makes something else happen.

- Corrie Ten Boom: Cornelia A. Johanna "Corrie" ten Boom (April 1892–April 1983) was a Dutch watchmaker and later a Christian writer and public speaker, who worked with her father, Casper ten Boom, her sister Betsie ten Boom and other family members to help many Jewish people escape from the Nazis during the Holocaust in World War II by hiding them in her home. Source: https://www.corrietenboom.com/en/foundation/organization

- Coup d'é·tat: a sudden decisive exercise of force in politics especially the violent overthrow or alteration of an existing government by a small group

- Glory Cloud of God: The Lord's glory cloud is what is called a theophany as defined by a visible manifestation to humankind of God. Also known as The Shekinah Glory. The word "Shekinah" was adopted by Christians as a way of describing God!s presence with His people. The phrase "Shekinah glory" is a symbol referring to that divine presence. God promised to "dwell among"

His people: "And there I will meet with you, and I will speak with you from above the mercy seat, from between the two cherubim which are on the ark of the Testimony" (Exodus 25:2) Source:https://www.bibleinfo.com/en/ questions/shekinah-glory

- Hymn. Count Your Blessings: Author Johnson Atman, 1897 Source: https://hymnary.org/text/when_upon_lifes_billows_you_are_tempest
- Hymn. Jesus Loves Me: Author: Anna Bartlett Warner Source: https://hymnary.org/text/jesus_loves_me_this_i_know_for_the_bible
- Hymn. I Believe in Miracles: Author: Carlton C. Buck and Music: John Willard Peterson. Source: https://hymnary.org/search? qu=i+believe+in+miracles
- Hymn: "Nobody Knows the Trouble I've Seen" is an African-American spiritual song that originated during the period of slavery published 1867. Source: https://hymnary.org/text/ sometimes_im_up_sometimes_im_down_oh_yes

- Jan Ruff O'Hearne: Awarded for outstanding service to the international community as an advocate for human rights and the protection of women in war, and for leadership in encouraging articulation of war-related atrocities. Source: https://www.wikidata.org/ wiki/Q11310259

- Kathryn Kuhlman: (1907 – 1976) was an American evangelist known for hosting healing services. Source: https://en.wikipedia.org/wiki/Kathryn_Kuhlman and https://www.christianlifeministries.com.au/ people-of-faith/kathryn-kuhlman/

- Oswald Chambers: (24 July 1874 – 15 November 1917) was an early- twentieth-century Scottish Baptist evangelist and teacher who was aligned with the Holiness Movement. He is best known for the daily devotional My Utmost for His Highest. Source: https://en.wikipedia.org/wiki/Oswald_Chambers

- Painting. Fitly by Denise R Dahlheimer
  Available @ https://artontheoutskirts.wixsite.com/home/product-page/fitly-prints-and-giclees

- Painting. Keep Going by Denise R Dahlheimer
  Available @ https://artontheoutskirts.wixsite.com/home/product-page/keep-going-prints-giclees

- Painting. Soliloquy by Denise R Dahlheimer
  Available @ https://artontheoutskirts.wixsite.com/home/product-page/soliloquy

- Painting. Rapture ~ Shakespeare by Sunflowers by Denise R Dahlheimer. Available @
  https://artontheoutskirts.wixsite.com/home/product-

# Trade Secrets of a Seer

page/shakespeare-by-sunflowers

- Play. The Merchant of Venice play by Shakespeare: The Merchant of Venice is a 16th-century play written by William Shakespeare in which a merchant in Venice named Antonio defaults on a large loan provided by a Jewish moneylender, Shylock. https://www.britannica.com/topic/ The-Merchant-of-Venice

- Song: Mama I am Coming Home, Ozzie Osbourne. https://www.allmusic.com/album/mama-im-coming-home-mw0000611759/credits

- Song: Wonderful World, Louis Armstrong. https://www.allmusic.com/artist/louis-armstrong-mn0000234518/credits

- Song: Smile., Uncle Kracker. https://genius.com/Uncle-kracker-smile-lyrics

- The Gifts of the Holy Spirit: 1 Corinthians 12 "1 Now concerning spiritual gifts, brethren, I do not want you to be ignorant: 2 You know that you were Gentiles, carried away to these dumb idols, however you were led. 3 Therefore I make known to you that no one speaking by the Spirit of God calls Jesus accursed, and no one can say that Jesus is Lord except by the Holy Spirit. 4 There are diversities of gifts, but the same Spirit. 5 There are differences of ministries, but the same Lord. 6 And there are diversities of activities, but it is the same God who works all in all. 7 But the manifestation of the Spirit is given to each one for the profit of all: 8 for to one is given the word of wisdom through the Spirit, to another the word of knowledge through the same Spirit, 9 to another faith by the same Spirit, to another gifts of healings by the same Spirit, 10 to another the working of miracles, to another prophecy, to another discerning of spirits, to another different kinds of tongues, to another the interpretation of tongues. 11 But one and the same Spirit works all these things, distributing to each one individually as He wills." Source: https://www.biblegateway.com/passage/?search=1+Corinthians+12&version=NKJV

- Trade Secrets definition quote: Source: https://www.winston.com/en/legal-glossary/trade-secret.html

Thank you for your time and interest. Be blessed!

www.ingramcontent.com/pod-product-compliance
Lightning Source LLC
Chambersburg PA
CBHW050252120526
44590CB00016B/2323